Governing Complex Societies

Also by Jon Pierre

CHALLENGES TO POLICY CAPACITY *(co-editor with Martin Painter, 2005)*

POLITICIZATION OF THE CIVIL SERVICE IN COMPARATIVE PERSPECTIVE *(co-editor with B. Guy Peters, 2004)*

HANDBOOK OF PUBLIC ADMINISTRATION *(editor, 2003)*

POLITICIANS, BUREAUCRATS AND ADMINISTRATIVE REFORM *(editor, 2001)*

DEBATING GOVERNANCE *(editor, 2000)*

GOVERNANCE, POLITICS AND THE STATE *(with B. Guy Peters, 2000)*

PARTNERSHIPS IN URBAN GOVERNANCE *(editor, 1998)*

Also by B. Guy Peters

AMERICAN PUBLIC POLICY *(6th edn, 2004)*

THE POLITICS OF BUREAUCRACY *(5th edn, 2001)*

COMPARATIVE POLITICS: Theory and Method *(2000)*

GOVERNANCE, POLITICS AND THE STATE *(with Jon Pierre, 2000)*

INSTITUTIONAL THEORY IN POLITICAL SCIENCE *(1999)*

Governing Complex Societies

Trajectories and Scenarios

Jon Pierre
Professor of Political Science
University of Gothenburg, Sweden

and

B. Guy Peters
Maurice Falk Professor of Government
University of Pittsburgh, USA

First published in 2005 by
PALGRAVE MACMILLAN
Houndmills, Basingstoke, Hampshire RG21 6XS and
175 Fifth Avenue, New York, N.Y. 10010
Companies and representatives throughout the world.

PALGRAVE MACMILLAN is the global academic imprint of the
Palgrave Macmillan division of St. Martin's Press, LLC and of
Palgrave Macmillan Ltd. Macmillan® is a registered trademark in the
United States, United Kingdom and other countries. Palgrave is a
registered trademark in the European Union and other countries.

ISBN-13: 978–1–4039–4660–4
ISBN-10: 1–4039–4660–4

A catalogue record for this book is available from the British Library.

Library of Congress Cataloging-in-Publication Data

Pierre, Jon.
    Governing complex societies : trajectories and scenarios / Jon Pierre
and B. Guy Peters.
        p. cm.
    Includes bibliographical references and index.
    ISBN 1–4039–4660–4 (cloth)
        1. Public administration. 2. Public administration—Europe.
    3. Public-private sector cooperation. 4. Democracy. I. Peters, B. Guy.
    II. Title.

JF1351.P54 2005
351'.01—dc22   2004060144

10 9 8 7 6 5 4 3 2 1
14 13 12 11 10 09 08 07 06 05

Contents

Acknowledgments

Our previous book on governance which was published in 2000 was in part intended to help put governance on the political science research agenda. While it remains highly unclear to what extent the book propelled the rapidly growing interest in the wide range of issues related to contemporary governance, it is clear that research in this field has become somewhat of an academic growth industry.

The previous book was mainly concerned with the transformation of the state as a result of such powerful changes as globalization, cut-back politics and subnational assertiveness on political and economic issues. Unlike some other observers, we maintained that what is happening is indeed a transformation of the state and its institutions, not necessarily a decline. This book picks up where the first book ended and is more focused on social, political, and economic complexity as causes or drivers of new, emerging models of governance.

Parts of the book have been presented at seminars and conferences; indeed, earlier versions of a couple of chapters have been published elsewhere. Ian Bache, Jean-Michel Eymeri, Matthew Flinders, Yannis Papadopolous, Bo Rothstein and Gerry Stoker have commented on early drafts of different chapters. The staff at Palgrave has been as helpful as ever. We should also thank the staff at United Airlines' Gold Lounge at Kingsford Smith Airport in Sydney for providing optimal conditions for reflecting on complexity, governance, and related issues.

Most importantly, we owe more than we can say to Sheryn Peters and Monika Pierre for snapping us out of excessive brooding on governance.

1
Understanding Governance: Institutional Capacity, Information, and Steering

Some time ago now, one of the present authors noted that "governance is a scarce commodity" (Peters, 2001:1). While that remains the case, the literature on governance certainly can no longer be described as scarce. During the past several years, issues related to governance have been rapidly gaining attention among academics as well as practitioners. It is not unfair to say that the debate on governance has, in an amazingly short period of time, developed into a large subfield of political science on both sides of the Atlantic as well as in many other parts of the world (Kjaer, 2004). At the same time many international organizations have been investing their time and money in attempts to create "good governance" in less well-governed societies (Kaufman, 2004).

Although widely used, the concept of governance is, however, far from precise and has taken on a number of alternative, and even contradictory, meanings in the literature. Much of the current debate on governance revolves around the role of political institutions in governance. The dominant line of skirmish separates a network perspective on governance in which the role of the state is negligible, if not irrelevant, from several approaches to governance in which the state, although now less powerful and omnipotent compared to a few decades ago, still dominates governance by controlling critical resources.

As is obvious later, our view falls into the latter governance school. That having been said, we believe that this key issue in governance research has not been properly addressed or structured. Further, we believe that in some ways the distinction made between the approaches to governance is a false dichotomy, and the most effective forms of governance require both social networks and a strong state (see Jessop, 2001). In an effort to sort out the underlying dimensions of the role of the state in governance, Chapter 2 presents five different models of governance, each with a slightly different conceptualization of the role of the state.

The approach we are taking to governance in this volume is somewhat more concerned with the role of society in the process than was true for our first book on governance theory. In this book we begin with the obvious yet often ignored point that the societies that governments seek to govern are extremely complex, and have become even more complex. Rather than ceding control to that complex and often incoherent society, as have some scholars, we are, in contrast, attempting to find ways to understand how governance can occur through the interplay of social and governmental action. There is, in this view, a clear role to be played by the state in steering the society, but that steering is always in the context of complexity and always in the context of bounded rationality and experimentation.

What is governance?

The first topic that must be addressed is just what do we mean when we use the term "governance" (see Pierre and Peters, 2000). For some scholars governance means little more than government—see for instance Osborne and Gaebler's (1991) notion of governance as "the business of government"—but has been a way of referring to the *process* and the *outcomes* rather than public sector institutions in and of themselves. The more challenging intellectual developments have come form those scholars who see governance as implying a much diminished role for formal institutions. For example, analysts such as Rosenau and Czempiel (1992) have argued that changes in the international environment have reduced government capacity to control policy outcomes. At even more of an extreme, Rhodes (1997) has argued that the contemporary public sector is characterized by "governance without government," meaning that governments have lost the capacity to govern their societies and that, to the extent that there is any meaningful control over social actors, it comes through networks and other self-referential structures. Governments may establish a legal framework within which those networks function but in this view the public sector does little more.

We are not negative about the capacity of governments to continue to govern. We understand that the public sector no longer governs society in what had been the conventional "command and control" manner, but yet it remains capable of participating in governance, and there are some components of governance for which government is as essential, or even more essential, than in the past. That role of government is all the more crucial for *democratic* governance, given the need to have some means for collective priority and preference setting (Hirst, 2000). Networks of voluntary action may be able to steer some aspects of policy, assuming that all members agree, but those networks are much less capable of coping either with disagreement among the members or with disagreements across policy sectors. Only governments are capable of resolving the more difficult problems of conflict resolution and comprehensive allocation of resources.

In particular, for the purposes of this book, we are using governance to represent the combined product of four classic activities that are components of governance. For each of these activities, political institutions have for some time been the dominant actors, although there has been a growing involvement by societal actors during the recent decades. The four activities in governance are:

(1) *Articulating a common set of priorities for society.* The first and perhaps most essential task for governance is articulating a set of priorities and goals for society that can be agreed upon by that society. This set of goals, in turn, provides the principal place for government (in the traditional sense) in governance. Perhaps no other set of institutions in society is capable of articulating collective priorities, especially in a democratic manner. The market, for example, provides a mechanism for exchange but assumes that sets of complementary and competitive goals are already in place. Likewise, networks may have common goals for their members but are not capable of setting goals more broadly.

Governance therefore refers to some mechanism or process through which a consensus, or at a minimum, a majority decision on social priorities and objectives can emerge. Such a process must logically include a mediating role exercised by institutions that are perceived as legitimate. While we are concerned primarily about governance within a democratic context some of the same characterization of governance and institutions would be relevant for nondemocratic systems. There must still be some mechanism for deciding upon goals, and in such settings the non-democratic sources of authority may be as valid in their context as are democratic institutions in other settings.

(2) *Coherence.* As well as having goals clearly articulated, there is a need for those goals to be consistent and coordinated. It may be possible to govern at a minimalist level through incoherent and unco-ordinated processes across policy sectors, but it will be inefficient and excessively costly. Much of that cost may be economic, but some also will be political. If citizens believe that their governing institutions are incapable of acting in a responsible manner they will tend to lose confidence in them, further exacerbating difficulties in governing. Given that authority and legitimacy make governing through rela-tively inexpensive instruments such as information more possible (Bemelmans-Videc *et al.*, 1998) then maintaining confidence is an important goal for governing institutions.

Again, networks and markets, as alternative forms of governance (Thompson *et al.*, 1991), are generally, not particularly, capable of cre-ating coherence, especially coherence across a large range of policy areas. The absence of goals that span those policy areas, and means of developing more overarching goals, limit the coordination capa-bilities of the alternatives to the state that are commonly advanced as alternatives to the state. Again, governments (and particularly the upper levels of government) are crucial for creating coherence (see, for instance, Peters *et al.*, 2000; Pressman and Wildavsky, 1974) given that they are meant to produce such a broad vision and balancing of interests. While often imperfect in providing that coherence, govern-ments may be the only real alternative.

(3) *Steering.* The third requirement for governance is a capacity for steering. Once a set of goals is established there is the need to find ways of achieving those goals and steering the society to attain those goals. The conventional means of governance has been for the public sector to use regulation, direct provision, and subsidies (among other policy instruments) to achieve those goals. As patterns of steering and policy implementation change, however, the instruments employed have been changing to include a number that involve working rela-tionships with private sector actors (see Salamon, 2000).

The nongovernmental actors have a better possibility of providing this dimension of governance than do the others. Both markets and networks are useful means of implementing programs. The market can be used when efficiency goals are paramount and when the program being implemented involves some possibilities of pricing and exchange. Networks have been useful when programs involve multiple actors from the private sector, especially when the service being delivered is not marketable and involves close interactions with clients. That having been said, for some public programs—especially those involving the basic rights of the participants—government itself may be the best source for implementation.

(4) *Accountability.* The final requirement for governance is some means of holding those actors delivering governance to the society to be accountable for their actions. Again, this requirement is a particular weakness for the nongovernmental actors involved in the governance process, given that markets in particular tend to have little or no concept of accountability. Contemporary governments have notable problems of implementing accountability (Chapman, 2000), but this concept remains deeply ingrained in the public sector.

Again, the concept of accountability is especially important for democratic governance. The complexity of policy, the fragmentation of political parties, and the limited capacity of the public to sanction or reward elected officials until the next election places a special burden on mechanisms of *ex post* accountability for contemporary democracy (Barberis, 1998; Klitgaard, 1988). Without well-designed and functioning means of accountability, democracy may have genuine difficulties in maintaining its commitments to the public. Even in nondemocratic systems, however, there are still demands for ensuring that the implementation of programs corresponds to the demands of the leadership.

The requirements for governing are formidable. Although there is substantial interest in providing "governance without government" in academic political science, it appears that governments must retain a central position in that activity. That position is not exclusive, but it is central. Further, attempts to eliminate government from governing may not only reduce the coherence of any governing that may be undertaken, but also reduce its democratic content. While there may be some scholars and citizens yearning for alternative governance structures—we need only think of communitarianism and deliberative models of democracy—we are still far from the emergence of any processes or institutions that could replace government in a democracy. To be sure, throughout the Western world, democracy without government as we know it is in essence unthinkable.

Understanding governance is basically a matter of understanding the nature of state–society relationships in the pursuit of collective interests. The four dimensions discussed here should be seen as arenas of such exchange. Also, understanding governance means understanding the political nature of governance. There is a tendency on the part of the governance literature to focus on the consensual and cosy deliberations in networks or other instruments of governance. We maintain, however, that governance is just another way of defining the role of government in society hence the analysis must be able to conceptualize and account for conflict regarding objectives and means. To be sure, a critical aspect of different models of governance is their ability to resolve conflict and generate consent among the key actors.

We should also point out that one of the virtues of the functionalist notions of governance advanced here is that, just as did earlier functionalist models in political science, it enables us to examine governing in a variety of settings. In particular, it permits us to look at governance occurring in poorly structured situations such as multilevel governance (MLG) in which there are numerous actors vying for control. By asking questions about how governance activities are performed, we can gain some answers about these processes even when the reality appears to diverge the stated conditions for governing.

State and society in governance

From the above discussion it is clear that state and society are both involved in governance, but there are a variety of ways in which the two sets of institutions interact to supply that all too scarce commodity (Rosenau, 2001). State and society interact in governance. This is true both conceptually and operationally. Conceptually, the discussion of the increased role of social actors in governance depends largely on an entrenched conceptualization that is heavily state-centric. More practically, the notion of networks and other societal actors supplying governance still depends on the capacity to enforce decisions in some ways, something that again implies the power of the public sector and its legitimate authority. On the other hand, the use of the private sector often is a means through which the public sector is able to legitimate its actions in an era of public distrust of government.

The mixtures of the influence of state and societal power vary substantially across countries, even among economically developed democracies, as does the particular manner in which the two sets of actors interact. Therefore, there is a need to explicate these alternative patterns, and to discuss the means through which they are able to supply governance. In the appropriate circumstances each pattern can be successful, and likewise each of the alternative arrangements can fail. The capacity of each to govern depends upon its conformity with social, economic, and political values and structures. Van Waarden (1995), for example, points to a number of systemic variations among political systems that are a function of the manner in which state and society interact.

The four aspects of governance discussed earlier—goal definition, coherence, steering, and accountability—have several features in common. First, all those activities appear to require a rather high degree of institutional capacity (Weaver and Rockman, 1993) if they are to be performed successfully. In this case institutional capacity refers to the availability of institutional resources such as staff, financial resources, professionalism and expertise, and so on, as well as to some sufficient level of trust in, and legitimacy for, the institution given by members of the surrounding society. One of the intriguing insights which arises from applying the governance perspective on political processes is that the strength of institutions—and, for that matter, the capacity of the state as a whole—is the joint outcome of institutional capacity, access to information, and some degree of consent and support from society (see Migdal, 1988).

Another aspect of institutional capacity is integrity. Institutions which become captives of parochial interests cannot make independent judgments in the interests of the polity as a whole. Institutional integrity is also necessary for making and implementing decisions that discriminate among constituencies, or simply decisions which are unpopular, but perhaps necessary, for the long-term prosperity of society. If we return to the first two fundamental activities in governance—goal setting and creating coherence—relatively autonomous and integral institutions appear crucial to being able to make decisions that move the society as a whole forward.

Furthermore, the ability of institutions to provide governance hinges on the availability of reliable information, and the ability to process information. Institutions need to know the societal effects of previous decisions; this is the classical feedback loop in systems models of political decision making (Deutsch, 1967). Information is also necessary for institutions in order to make decisions which are appropriate, given the nature of the problem which is to be resolved. Information is best acquired if the institution has several points of contact with society through which information can be communicated to decision makers. Any single channel may become clogged or miss crucial information, so that redundancy may benefit government.

As we discuss in more detail later in subsequent chapters, there exists a tension, if not an outright conflict, between institutional capacity and access to information. Textbook examples of "strong states" like France display institutions with extensive capacity (see, for example, Hayward, 1983) for autonomous action. However, they lack the broad interface with society that provides the state with information about societal problems or the outcome of previous policy. Similarly, states that have a large number of channels of exchange with society tend to have institutions that lack the integrity to formulate and implement policy effectively. These institutions also have a problem with ensuring coherent and accountable governance; coherence is lost because of the lack of overview and accountability is confused because state institutions are not in control. It is important that we remember these goal conflicts as we continue our analysis to discuss different models of governance.

Organization of the book

The basic organizing idea in the book is to first elaborate different empirical and analytical models of governance. From there—and largely drawing on similar analytical perspectives—we focus on different models of multilevel governance and finally raise questions about legitimacy and accountability in governance. Thus, Chapter 2 compares five different models of governance. The five models are placed on a continuum from an étatiste model dominated by the state to the "governance without government" perspective which assumes a minimalist state. The five models, and especially the two ends of the continuum, border upon ideal types, but yet are useful in understanding governance, and demonstrate the utility of governance ideas in comparative politics.

The next several chapters highlight different aspects and problematic associated with multilevel governance. Chapter 3 applies a garbage can theoretical model to multilevel governance. Garbage can theory, with its bounded rationality approach to decision making, has a lot to offer in terms of understanding governance processes. We apply the multilevel governance theory to the European Union (EU) in Chapter 4. The EU is frequently used almost as a standard case of multilevel governance, and we demonstrate how that analytic idea works within the EU. We structure our analysis along three dimensions of multilevel governance; time, space, and structure. While this might sound slightly metaphysical, the three dimensions are used to define process, levels, and institutions.

Chapter 5 asks to what extent the informal, almost cosy, nature of multilevel governance masks diverging interests and potential conflict. Is it the case that the flexibility and informality which is typical to multilevel governance, in fact, is a model of governance which favors the interests of the stronger actor at the expense of the weaker players?

It seems clear, on reflection, that multilevel governance is still largely conducted along traditional institutional lines. Just as we repeatedly emphasize the importance of institutions in governance throughout the book, we believe this to be the case also in multilevel governance. Thus, Chapter 6 looks at recent changes in Western Europe against the backdrop of the multilevel governance model. Much of the multilevel governance literature is fairly quiet on the role of institutions in these types of processes. However, as we find that institutions matter a great deal in governance at individual levels, it appears only logical to assume that they structure much of multilevel governance as well.

Chapter 7 addresses the issues of legitimacy and democracy in contemporary governance. Again, we find that institutions matter in governance, not least because institutions remain the undisputed structures of representation and accountability. This arrangement also provides institutions with legitimacy. How is legitimacy sustained in complex patterns of governance? How do we know that governance is democratic?

A concluding chapter consolidates the themes and arguments developed in the preceding chapters. We also point to the research agenda that governance presents for political science. In particular, we show how these ideas can be used as a means of organizing comparative political research.

2
Toward a Theory of Governance

In Chapter 1, we defined the key dimensions of governance; articulating collective goals and priorities, ensuring coherence, steering, and accountability. It almost goes without saying that the precise nature of the process through which these governance roles of the state evolve cannot be postulated in very much detail. In order to be able to say something about the process, we need to consider different analytical models of exchange between state and society. We argue that there are five fundamental models of state and society interactions in governance that are now operating among contemporary democratic systems. These models all require both social and public sector actors in order to perform their tasks, but see those actors employed in different ways and with varying strength.

These models represent varying means of coping with the problem of complexity discussed earlier. They also represent different political histories and state traditions. Governing does not occur on a *tabula rasa* but rather it reflects adaptations that have been learned over decades if not centuries (Dyson, 1980; Olsen and Peters, 1996). At times governments have learned their lessons too well and have institutionalized patterns that in the first part of the twenty-first century may be inefficient means for coping. In particular, governing models that minimize the capacity for countries to absorb and act on information coming from society appear less viable than those that are more open to information. That openness must, however, be balanced against the capacity to make decisions in a prompt and decisive manner.

For each of the model we discuss the actors involved, the nature of the processes and political dynamics, and the outcomes of the processes. Also for each we argue that there is a set of fundamental characteristics that differentiates it from the others. Thus, we argue that there are some important commonalities in governance but there are also some crucial differences. Further, these five models constitute a continuum ranging from the most dominated by the state and those in which the state plays the least role and indeed one in which there is argued to be governance without government.

The five models of governance that we investigate are:

(1) *Étatiste*. This is perhaps the basic model against which the "governance without government" advocates are reacting. The assumption is that government is the principal actor for all aspects of governance and can control the manner in which the social actors are permitted to be involved, if they are at all. This model is in many ways the constitutional doctrine for Westminster governments, although the reality is often quite different, but again this is a source of the seeming extreme reaction of some scholars (see Rhodes *et al.*, 1997).

(2) *Liberal-democratic*. The liberal-democratic model accepts the role of the state as the principal actor in governance. Other actors compete to influence the state, but the state has the opportunity to pick and choose the interest groups or other social actors that it will *permit* to have influence. Thus, the state is not totally shielded from influence by society but neither does it accept the legitimate right of a range of interests to participate. This model maintains a strong commitment to representative democracy, in contrast to some below that focus increasingly on other forms of democratic involvement of social actors.

(3) *State-centric*. As we move through this continuum the third step is labeled state-centric. The state remains at the center of the process, but institutionalizes its relationships with social actors. Thus, various forms of corporatism and formalized state–society relationships fit into this model. The state has substantial powers in accepting or rejecting partners, but is yet more bound to its partners than would be true for the previous two models. As state–society interactions are transforming, "softer" versions of this model are becoming predominant, usually phrased in terms of the civil society (Perez-Diaz, 1995; Putnam *et al.*, 1993), but the corporatist model remains the archetype of this pattern of governing.

(4) *The Dutch governance school.* The title of this model appears perhaps idiosyncratic, but it reflects the development of a particular approach to governance among Dutch scholars (Kickert, 1996; Kooiman, 1993), and perhaps also in the reality of Dutch politics.[1] This model depends heavily upon the role of social networks in governing, with the state being merely one among many actors involved in the process. In this approach society may in fact be the more powerful actor, given its capacity to organize itself to evade the power of the state and its attempts at regulation.

(5) *Governance without government.* Finally, there are those scholars who argue that the state has lost its capacity to govern and is at best an arena within which private actors play out their own interests to create more or less self-steering governance arrangements. Further, it is argued, as the state has been losing its legitimacy in society these actors actually have greater legitimacy than does the state and hence public sector actors could be argued to be less relevant to the process than are the social actors. The empirical referents for this model are found primarily in Northern Europe, although the implication has been that this model of governing is increasingly becoming a reality even for Westminster systems.

These five models represent an attempt to capture a rather complex reality within the confines of a relatively small number of alternative models. Still, we do believe that these five models capture a good deal of that complexity and demonstrate the range of interactions of state and society. Further, as the five are elaborated in this chapter the models enable us to understand better governance as a process and a set of outcomes, and to understand in comparative context the variety of ways in which societies have been found to govern themselves.

Characteristics of the models

The following is a very brief description of the basic building blocks of these models of governance, with the range of options that might exist for each of the categories. This preliminary discussion is intended only to point to some of the important analytical dimensions that are explored in greater depth in the descriptions of the five models themselves.

Actors

We have already pointed out that the two principal actors in each of the models are state and society. That simple dichotomy, however, masks a great deal of underlying complexity. This complexity is particularly important for the role of the state. In much of the literature on the state there is a tendency to treat the state as a unified actor, and to act as if there is a single entity involved in the political process. In reality, that is not the case in many, if not most, cases. There are numerous divisions within the state, with the most important usually being the ministerial "stovepipes" defined by policy areas (Peters, 2000b). Governments may also be divided by levels of government, with contemporary ideas concerning "multi-level governance" (see Peters and Pierre, 2004; Pierre and Stoker, 2000; and the literature cited therein) pointing out the need to bring together several levels of government in order to produce a relatively coherent set of policies. There are strong pressures to create more coherent styles of governing both within and across levels of government, but it is still appropriate in most instances to think of a more divided state.

Just as the state is a differentiated actor so too is society. This differentiation is perhaps more easily understood than is that argued to exist for the state, given that we understand that there are often a series of competing interests in society that attempt to use the state as the arena for achieving their ends. Further, as we discuss social networks later, the indeterminacy of the outcomes of these social structures means that there is a need to specify how they operate and the manner in which social actors make decisions on their own, or participate in public sector decision making. While the state may be divided into "stovepipes," private sector actors within each policy area are themselves often divided and seek different outcomes. Thus, as we discuss society as an actor in governance, we need to exercise some care in our assumption of how "society" and its various components will perform.

Again, we return to the theme of complexity, indicating that there is substantial social and policy complexity, and that this is to some extent mirrored structurally within government. The governance task, therefore, is to create some capacity for action in the midst of all the barriers and the divisions, and in the presence of uncertainty. The capacity to interpret prior actions and to respond effectively to them therefore becomes central to governance capacity. This is all the more relevant as both state and society become more complex, the problems become perhaps less clearly defined, and hence uncertainty is greater. As one simple example, much of the literature about the relationship between state and society is focused on societal actors based primarily on economic interests and, while those interests certainly persist, they have been joined by a host of other ethnic, regional, gender, and lifestyle considerations that make predictions of outcomes and the politics leading up to those outcomes more difficult.

Processes

The process of providing governance to society involves a number of steps, not dissimilar to the familiar "stages" model of the policy process (Jones, 1982; Peters, 1999). Like the stages model this enumeration of processes has at its heart a notion that authoritative decisions must be made that allocate values for the society, as in the famous Easton definition of politics. The principal difference is that governance does not have the public sector bias that the policy literature displays, or at least is more willing to admit that the private sector may have a crucial role to play in the creation of governance.

Goal selection

The first, and in some ways most crucial, aspect of governance is identifying the collective goals of society. The analogous part of the policy process is problem identification and agenda setting. The important difference in the governance context is that this is a more normative process, with the crucial element being to decide *what* society wants, rather than deciding simply which issues will be processed at any particular time. As already noted, this stage tends to be highly governmental, given that this may be the only legitimate means of collective action for the society.

Decision making

The next part of the governance process is making decisions about how to reach the goals that have been established. This function too is often performed within the public sector, albeit generally with a good deal of input from the private sector. This involves, among other things, the selection of instruments and the selection of a mix of public and private action that is deemed most appropriate for reaching the goals.

Resource mobilization

Although closely associated with decision making, resource attachment implies the need to identify and mobilize public and private resources to reach the goals. Thus, a particular set of instruments may have been adopted but if there are not the resources necessary to make them work then those instruments are almost certain to be ineffective. Also, although financial resources are a crucial element, personnel and perhaps most importantly legitimacy are also important elements of the resource base for governance.

Instruments/implementation

The implementation process is a crucial component of the governance process, although it is sometimes relegated to "mere administration." We noted earlier that the choice of instruments is part of decision-making in governance, and at the implementation stage these instruments are made to perform and to produce the effects intended. These instruments (even in more state-centric models) often depend upon private sector actors so that this can also be a point at which there is substantial loss of control over policies.

Feedback

The final part of the governance process is feedback, with the actions of instruments in the past being evaluated and put back into the decision-making process. Governance has the same root word as "cybernetics" and hence implies some connection to the environment and a continual adjustment of instruments (and perhaps even goals) in light of the success and failure of actions taken in the past. The feedback function generally must be initiated by social actors and then be brought into the governing process. The state, however, must be receptive to that feedback, and must have the mechanism to receive and to process it. Given that society itself is increasingly complex, and to some extent also more capable, managing feedback becomes more difficult intellectually, even as communications technology makes it somewhat easier technically.

Outcomes

Finally, we should examine the outcomes of the governance process. Just as government has policy as its principal outcome, governance has as its primary concern the outcomes of the process. In this case, however, we are not as concerned with specific policies as with broader characteristics of the policies adopted. These ideas about governing reflect the more summary nature of governance, and the need to consider a more comprehensive set of outcomes.

Coherence

Governments are highly fragmented institutions and must consider a broad range of issues. One governance challenge faced is to put together that range of policies and, along with that, a huge range of policy goals into a coherent governance package. This challenge arises at the stage of goal setting and policy formulation, and also arises at the implementation stage as multiple policies are put into effect and require coordination. The failure to achieve coherence among its policies can be a severe problem for governance, given that it not only generates excessive costs but also presents an image of incompetence to the public.

Inclusiveness

The term inclusiveness has several meanings. On the one hand, it implies the need to bring together a range of interests and to ensure that important social elements are not excluded from policies. It also implies the need to include both state and society in governance. Both ends of the continuum of models discussed later are exclusive, while models in the middle are more inclusive. In those models both state and society must cede some power in order to govern more effectively.

Adaptability

Another crucial dimension of governance is the capacity of governing systems to respond effectively to changes in the challenges presented by the external environment, or by changes within the governance arrangements themselves. One major driver of change in contemporary governance is globalization that forces reexamination of conventional approaches to governing and also links policies in ways that might not otherwise occur. Technological change also may bring into question traditional policy approaches. In short, governance is likely to be more problematic in the immediate future.

Accountability

Finally, accountability is a central assessment criterion for governance. We mentioned this as a central requirement for governance earlier, and we bring it back here to point to it as a crucial outcome of the process. This outcome is closely linked with the process of feedback. Accountability may involve both public and the private sector actors, although ultimately it must depend upon the authority of the public sector to enforce findings of inadequate performance of the governance regime.

Models of governance

We now move to a more detailed discussion of the five alternative models of governance mentioned earlier. Given limitations of time and space even these must be rather sketchy descriptions, but even so, these discussions should point to the alternative means of governing. Further, these models are just that, and border on being ideal types. Therefore, we need to be sensitive to the cases that do not fall neatly into the five models, and be cognizant that few if any national cases will fit perfectly into any of the models. Still, these models provide a way to organize thinking about the issues.

The étatiste model

The first model is the étatiste model, based on the capacity of the state to govern with little or no involvement of societal actors. In contemporary democratic societies such a pattern of governance may appear unlikely, as indeed it is, but some industrialized countries do verge on this model. Further, historically this has been a crucial way of governing and in the contemporary period has been typical of many industrializing countries such as Singapore and Taiwan that have used state power as a means of facilitating economic development (Evans, 1995).

Actors

The principal actor in this model is, rather obviously, the state. The state need not, however, be a unitary actor and the governance that emerges from the étatiste version of governance may be as incoherent as that coming from any of the others. Indeed, organizational analysis may be a central means of understanding the manner in which the state performs in this model, with top leadership in the state attempting to control a large number of organizations that pursue their own interests. That having been said, there is some point at which the overall interests of the state may conflict with the interests of individual organizations, so that the top leadership would be forced to intervene to coordinate and create policy coherence. Further, the strong states implied by this model tend to have the capacity to pull themselves together when required and to present themselves to society as coherent and integrated actors that can govern effectively, and can do so without the society providing any assistance.

If the state and its organizations do choose to interact with society, those interactions are on its own terms, rather than with any sense of equality with social organizations. Rather than consulting in a genuine manner, interactions with society may be used to legitimate actions in an apparently democratic manner. This generally means that the state will dominate the goal selection process even more than other aspects of governance so that it can use raison d'etat as the justification for its activity. This becomes the normative stance that controls policy choice and their implementation. Among the developed democracies, France (but see Ashford, 1982) may come as close to this model of governing as any other country, although it too has been forced to modernize its approach in light of both pressures toward modernization and pressures from EU membership.

Processes

The étatiste model of governing has, not surprisingly, the state as a central actor in all policy processes. The centrality of the state and its organizations may mean that these processes appear more efficient than processes in the models later. That is, given that the state is capable of controlling access it can make decisions and move issues through the processes more readily than can systems in which social actors are capable of exerting independent influences.

Goal selection. As noted, goal selection tends to be the process of governance that may be the most dominated by the state, even in more societally dominated systems. That state domination is all the more apparent in this étatiste model. In this model the state has the capability of defining goals in terms of its view of social needs, although this may be done without the society itself being accorded the opportunity to participate. Further, if the state is wrong there is little capacity for the state to correct itself, given that it is receiving only limited social intelligence, and only that intelligence that it wants to receive. Indeed the state may eschew even readily available social intelligence, believing that it knows better what is required for successful governance, and may not even have categories and ministerial structures to process information that members of society might consider crucial.

Perhaps the major institutions for social linkage for the state in this model of governance are political parties, especially hegemonic political parties. The dominant political party may be a source of policy and governance ideas, but those ideas are still mediated primarily through state organizations and may reflect the interest of those public organizations. Thus, state organizations may be able to control the agenda of even powerful political parties, and particularly are able to control the policy advice and the information available to decision makers. Few political parties will have the capacity to provide its members with the independent sources of information required to counteract the power of state organizations.

Decision making. The principal style of decision making in étatiste governance is technocratic. There is an assumption that policy decisions are subject to technical and "rational" policy analysis, and therefore do not require any significant involvement of social actors. As implied by the point on goal setting earlier, the state can become virtually autistic, receiving little information and losing touch with the relevant environment.

In the étatiste model, decision making (and much of the remainder of the governance process) is dominated by a political elite and a "political class." While there tends to be a political elite in all countries the important difference is in the extent of control exerted by this elite in making decisions. There are two other relevant points here. First, the state tends to play a dominant role in the formation of that elite, rather than having it arise through normal social and political processes. In addition, the elite tends to be more technocratic than in other styles of governing. Again the French example fits well with this model. The state, through its *grands écoles*, tends to be crucial in elite formation. Further, many of these écoles are technocratic, with schools such as the Polytechnique having a continuing role in defining the political elite.

Resource mobilization.   The state is a more active force in driving the economy in this model of governance than in others. Indeed, the state generally functions as a major, if not the major, entrepreneur as well as taxman, and may derive a significant proportion of its resources from production and finance. If, for example, we return to the example of France, the state was crucial in economic development and that mercantilist tradition continues, if in a diminished form, until this day (Hayward, 1986). The same is certainly true for state institutions in the majority of the newly industrialized countries (NICs) during the contemporary period and that role has been attempted less successfully in many developing countries (Evans, 1995). The state then is a major player in most aspects of social and economic life in the étatiste model and therefore provides little room for autonomous action by social actors.

State activity in resource mobilization is expected and legitimate in these systems. The state is understood to be a major economic actor and indeed if it did not play such a role it would be assumed to be shirking its responsibilities. Therefore, the failure of the state to remain in close contact with the economy and society may be even more problematic than it would be if the state were a less significant economic force. If the state fails to code important information as relevant for its actions, it is often incapable of making adequate decisions and frequently continues along well-worn paths that have diminishing returns as the economy and society change. Thus, paradoxically, the power of the étatiste model may allow the state to continue to make poor policies without challenge and hence may be much less effective and more open systems.

Instruments.   The étatiste model also depends upon a particular mix of policy instruments. In general this model employs a higher proportion of coercive and direct policy instruments than do the other models of governance. As already noted, the state is expected to intervene to a degree unacceptable in other models and therefore using more coercive instruments is simply a part of governing. It may be, in fact, that attempts to use less direct and intrusive instruments would undermine legitimacy rather than support it as those instruments do in most other governance styles. Using indirect and incentive-based instruments might be conceptualized as the state shirking its responsibilities. Further, the state tends to use a limited array of instruments to achieve its purposes (Peters, 2001b). The same instruments, generally direct provision of services and regulation, tend to be used in almost all circumstances.

In the étatiste model the state government institutions tend to implement their own policies rather than depending upon other actors for those activities. Again, attempts of the state to devolve implementation to other actors might well be considered inappropriate in the étatiste conception of governing. As a consequence the state continues to be more of public employer and to have additional economic consequences for society through this function. Not only is the state the principal actor in implementation but it also tends to press toward uniformity and homogeneity in the process. Therefore, in France and other Napoleonic states there is a great emphasis on creating uniformity through institutions such as prefects (Peters, 2001a).

Feedback.   Again, the state in the étatiste model tends to be little concerned with the role and utility of feedback from society. The dominant assumption is that the state knows best and will be able to adjust its own activities in order to govern more effectively, assuming any such adjustment is required. In some ways the state structure itself helps overcome the possible limitations of effective social feedback, given that the state has a large field staff of its own. With that internal structure the state may be more closely linked with social conditions than it would in the other, more disaggregated, models of governance. The intelligence the state receives may be more biased and less systematic than feedback available in other models, but there is at least some source of societal information available.

Outcomes

As we move to an examination of the outcomes of governing in the étatiste model, some of the inherent strengths and weaknesses of the approach become more apparent. Again, the nature of governing in this approach is somewhat paradoxical. On the one hand, the state has substantial strength and can do much of what it wants to do, and on the other hand, it may be blinded by that power and incapable of responding to changes in economy and society. In addition, the state may think of its activity as coordinated and of itself as a unitary actor while in reality there will be significant internal conflict and substantial incoherence.

Coherence.   Coherence might be thought to be a major strength of the étatiste mode of governance. Given that the state itself is the only real actor in the process, there should be no real problem of governing coherently. The reality, however, is otherwise and coherence is a major problem for this model. Further, given the absence of external checks on governing there are perhaps even greater problems in this model than in others. There are few of the political checks and balances that may push the political system toward greater coherence within the other styles of governing.

One major source of incoherence in étatiste governance is the presence of institutional turf fights that occur within the state itself. Rather than being a unified actor the state is actually divided along a number of dimensions, perhaps most importantly, divisions along functional lines and policy sectors. While there is an overall state elite and that elite may be socially integrated, there is often a good deal of division based upon the particular group being served and the type of expertise possessed by the members of government institutions. For example the technical, engineering elite in a developmental state may feel that it has little in common with the actors who deliver social policy or elementary education. Further, the style of governing often has been to divide and conquer, and to create *droits acquises* in society.

Inclusiveness.   Including a range of social actors is not one of the strong suits of étatiste governance, and as already noted involving society may actually be considered a negative in this model. If the state possesses the majority of the needed technical expertise within the system then trying to take in information from other sources may actually be counterproductive. The one way in which the state in the étatiste model will attempt to involve society is when it wishes to do so for strategic purposes. That is, the state may accord some rights of participation to a selected segment of society in order to be able to exert control over that segment, rather than listen to it. This style of governing was seen rather clearly in Franco's Spain (Anderson, 1968) in the creation of *parantela* relationships, and to a less extreme version in similar relationships in Italy.

Adaptability. The absence of effective feedback and social linkages limits the adaptive capacity of the state in the étatiste model. The state almost always operates with a severe information deficiency, even if it has information sources of its own. This is because such feedback as the state can receive is from its own, and probably highly biased, sources and contrary information will tend to be filtered out, wittingly or unwittingly, by those institutions. The state therefore has limited benefit of feedback and hence is not able to steer itself effectively, even to react to the success and failure of its own interventions into society.

Such a characterization of information use within the étatiste state raises a major paradox about governance for this group of states. On the one hand, the state has tremendous adaptive capacity, given that it confronts relatively few competitors for control coming from the society, and has a large reservoir of legitimacy to override any possible competitors. On the other hand, however, the étatiste state has limited means for identifying socioeconomic changes and understanding that it may need to adapt. Thus, the seemingly powerful state becomes a victim of its own power and its own abilities to restrict access to its locus of decision.

Accountability. Finally, we come to accountability and its role in governance. In the étatiste model accountability is largely internalized. Just as the state dominated its own collection and utilization of information, so too does the state control the way in which its actions are judged and evaluated. The usual concept of accountability involves some autonomous check on actions, but in the étatiste state that does not appear permissible. The state uses its own institutions and therefore limits the types and sources of information utilized for accountability purposes. The dominance of technocratic elites in the policy process in most étatiste states strengthens the autonomy of the state and further limits the capacity of other actors to exert accountability. Again, France can function as the best example of this style of governing among the industrialized democracies. Most of the accountability structures, for example, the Cours de Comptes, the Inspection des Finances, and the Conseil d'Etat are themselves state organizations and indeed are very central state institutions. While certainly the Napoleonic model of administration attempts to separate these administrative functions from other mundane actors who are being supervised (Wunder, 1995), there is still not the autonomy and independence for accountability systems that would be considered crucial in most political systems.

Summary

The picture of the étatiste style of government that we have been painting here may appear to be an overstatement and a stereotype, but we would consider it more as an ideal type. As is well known, this methodological approach does not assume that any perfect example of this model does exist or will exist in the real world. Rather the model is an intellectual construct against which to compare reality. We have been using the example of France throughout this discussion, but there are certainly elements of the French case that do not fit easily with this model. Still this, and the other models, are useful bases to begin the analysis of governance systems and the alternative ways in which governance can be supplied.

The liberal-democratic state and governance

The second stop along the continuum of governance models is the liberal-democratic state. Given the pluralist notions that reside at the heart of this model placing it so near the end of the continuum may appear mistaken. We argue, however, that this mode for organizing governance does attach a good deal of power to the state and uses society more than it permits society to exercise autonomous controls over policy. There is a symbiosis at the heart of this governance model, but it is a mutualism defined largely by the interests of the state and its need to coopt social actors for its own purposes.

Actors

Again, the principal actor in this model is the state. The state here is perhaps no longer the haughty entity we encountered in the first of these models, but it is still the dominant player in the governance process. The fundamental difference from the étatiste model is that in the liberal-democratic state the state is more an arena for action than a technocratic decision maker. The state will continue to make authoritative decisions, but will do so with some involvement of (organized) societal interests. Interestingly, in some cases the form of involvement of the nonstate actors may appear to accord them a great deal of influence, with certain interests being selected to act in the name of the state in a particular policy area.

The nonstate actors involved in policy making will themselves be in a competitive game, or perhaps a political marketplace, each attempting to exert influence on state action. In this game the state, or more properly state organizations or institutions, will pick and choose among the competitive groups and select those groups that have goals and values most in conformity with those of the state organization (see Van Waarden, 1995: 338). If no such appropriate group exists then the state may choose to propagate such a societal organization, usually in the form of an apparently autonomous interest group. That autonomy, will, of course, be more apparent than real. In fact, somewhat paradoxically, the more competition there is for state acceptance of competitive interests the more the state increases its own autonomy and is capable of structuring its own role and its policies. In this model of governance the state will be at least as divided as that discussed in the étatiste mode earlier. We might expect somewhat stronger internal division, in fact, given that organizations within the state will be linked to societal interests and those interests will seek to utilize their linkages to state actors to further policy goals. This colonization and symbiosis among actors will tend to fragment institutions both politically and in terms of their commitments to particular programs and methodologies of delivering policies. While there may be limited political pressures favoring coordination and coherence in this model, these tend to be overwhelmed by divisive, sectoral forces.

Processes

The processes of making policies will reflect the above characterization of the actors involved. The state and its component organizations remain central in these processes, but there is now some involvement of social interests. This greater inclusiveness will make the processes somewhat less determinate than in the étatiste model, although state organizations retain much of their capacity to control outcomes and to exclude almost any external actor that they may wish.

Goal selection.   As the state in this model is substantially more open, societal interests are conceptualized as having more role in the policy process, perhaps especially at the goal selection stage. This is a more political aspect of the policy process than many others, involving determination of broad patterns of policy. This stage will be more competitive in this version of governance than in the étatiste model. That competition will be among social groups (including political parties) that want to impose their own views on the state. Competition for the opportunity to participate also will occur between state organizations themselves, given that the state itself is highly segmented. Thus various components of the state will want to have their own sets of goals emphasized in the process. Thus, they are competing for budgetary resources and legislative time. Even more than the étatiste model then, this is the world of bureaucratic politics given that there is not the centralized authority and strength of the state to control that competition, and given that the state institutions are directly linked to societal institutions that are not without political resources of their own.

Decision making.   There is a certain duality in the role played by the state in decision making in this model. On the one hand, state organizations and institutions are active participants in the process of making decisions. There are other forms of politics but internal state politics are still crucial in making policy choices. Thus institutional interests are crucial for explaining policies. On the other hand, the state represents an arena within which those institutional interests and societal interests interact and combine to combat potentially hostile interests, with again much of this competition being over the budget. Further, in this style of making decisions, it is difficult to separate the interests of state institutions from the interests of the social actors. Again, the symbiosis of state and society is crucial for understanding politics within this model. This linkage of state and society also helps to produce distributive outcomes, with all or almost all interests receiving some benefits.

Resource mobilization.   The strength of segmented interests in state and society can help explain resource mobilization in this model. Resource mobilization follows the same distributive outcomes, as do the policy decisions described earlier. In this model all segments of society tend to pay something, just as they all will receive something. The state tends to opt for multiple revenue sources, with the state continuing to have some entrepreneurial income but mostly it depends upon multiple taxes. With those multiple sources of taxation all segments of society tend to share at least a part of the burden of financing the state. The relative strength of societal groups determines actual distribution of those burdens. Also, there is some tendency to utilize less visible sources of revenue in order to disguise winners and losers in the process.

Instruments/implementation.   The state in this model tends to implement many of its programs through societal actors and through self-regulatory devices. In short, the symbiosis that tends to characterize other aspects of the model is evident in the implementation of policy. One strategy that is utilized in attempting to maintain that symbiotic relationship is to employ the least coercive policy instruments possible, a factor that also conforms to many national political cultures that attempt to minimize the coercive nature of the state. Therefore, rather than direct imposition of government programs, those programs may be implemented through third-parties and through regulatory and self-regulatory instruments. Again, this implementation strategy tends to disguise winners and losers in the policy process, just as it does in the selection of policies at earlier stages.

Feedback.   The state in this model is more likely to accept and even encourage feedback, unlike the state in the étatiste model of governance. That feedback, however, is likely to be incomplete, reflecting the fragmentation of the policy process that we demonstrated earlier. The institutions—state as well as societal—that are attempting to use the policy process to advance their own interests would not hesitate to use the feedback process to further those interests. Therefore, the feedback that emerges in this system is likely to be biased and to reflect those interests. On the other hand, however, the feedback process here does have the advantage of coming from multiple sources—state and society—so that it may not be so biased as in the étatiste model. Feedback here may therefore be more representative of society than feedback in the former model.

Outcomes

We now proceed to examine the outcomes of this governance process, looking at the ways in which state and society interact in order to produce the policies of the state. This then is, to some degree, an assessment of the governance capacity of this model, just as similar analyses are for the other models.

Coherence.   The first outcome is how coherent are the outcomes of the process, and the degree of coordination that exists among the policies being adopted and implemented. As might be expected from the earlier description, coherence is not one of the stronger features of this model. Elites in this model are largely competitive, so that they are not likely to cooperate effectively in making policies in one policy area that conform well with those in other areas. The distributional outcomes that characterize the policy process are almost by definition not well coordinated, but rather reflect the power of each individual political group. In this approach to governance, consent is being purchased at the price of coherence. This may be a good political trade-off but perhaps is less good in policy terms than would be the more difficult task of creating policy coherence.

Inclusiveness.   Rather than be fully open and democratic, politics in this model of governance is oligopolistic, and is more of a cartel than a free market. Certainly, more actors are involved in governing than would be in the étatiste model, but these actors are there largely at the sufferance of the state. If it deems it necessary, the state can curtail or terminate involvement by the social actors. The state remains the principal legitimate actor in the process and therefore has the opportunity to select which players will be permitted and which will not. This selective inclusiveness of actors, and the tendency to select only "tame" interests from society means that decisions remain largely under the control of state actors.

Adaptability. In some ways this model of governance may be the least adaptable of the five, having as it does to a great extent the worst of both worlds. That is, by being more open the state loses some capacity to adapt as it sees fit, as in the étatiste model already discussed. On the other hand, society is not sufficiently autonomous to provide uncontaminated feedback to the state, nor to operate on its own to produce adaptations without involvement of the state. Further, adaptability is limited by the absence of any consensus about the direction in which to adapt. The divisions existing within the state may produce multiple visions about what the future should be. Likewise, these divisions are associated with differential pressures on organizations and policy sectors to adapt. This may mean that the state develops in unbalanced ways, with some policy areas being able to adapt and others being held back from effective change.

Accountability. Finally, we come to that crucial outcome of governance, accountability. In the liberal-democratic model there are multiple channels of accountability so that citizens have a number of ways in which they can attempt to hold the state accountable. Unlike the étatiste model, state and society have some direct linkages, both for political parties and for interest groups, in this approach to governance. Although these multiple channels do have some virtues for citizens, they can also be the source of some confusion. On the one hand, the state retains the ultimate capacity to pursue its own interests (or at least those of individual organizations) and can do so with a good deal of legitimacy. On the other hand, the dominant accountability system emphasizes partisan roles and the role of interest groups as representatives of segments of society. In short, it is not always clear who is being held accountable for what in this version of governance.

Summary

The liberal-democratic system of governance moves that activity away from the almost complete domination of the process by the state toward some form of cooperation between the public and private sectors in steering society. That cooperation is, however, asymmetric with the state retaining the dominant position. In particular, the state retains the capacity to determine which private sector organizations will be considered the appropriate representatives of their social sectors and hence which are acceptable partners for involving in governance. These social actors are linked into the state in highly segmented manners so that the state has less capacity to act as a single entity than might be expected from its generalized position of strength.

The state-centric governance model

The third model of governance we explore is entitled the "state-centric" approach. This title might lead one to believe that this model is actually closer to the étatiste model than is the liberal-democratic model but this version of governance differs in one important respect—in what we refer to as the state-centric model social interests have a legitimate right to participate and to have their ideas considered by the state. The state remains the central actor and the central decision maker but it is not able to make those decisions entirely on its own. Some form of negotiation is required and that is intended to align policies with both particular social interests and the collective concerns of society, as interpreted by the institutions of the state. The state also retains some capacity to determine who the participants from the private sector will be, but will have to accept some form of involvement of interests in policy making.

Actors

As already noted the state and its organizations remain at the center of governing in this model. The arena for making decisions is far from open but rather reflects the capacity of the state to mold that arena and play a decisive role in picking social actors. One way to understand this model of governing is through the perspective of corporatist politics as described by Schmitter (1974), with the state selecting official, exclusive representatives of social sectors. Even in more open versions of corporatist politics, for example, the corporate pluralism of Scandinavia (Kristensen and Johansen, 1983; Olsen, 1987) the state retains some capacity to determine who are appropriate representatives and who are not.

The latitude of the state is not, however, complete. These governing systems constitute opportunity structures for social actors who must then determine whether the opportunities presented are adequate to induce involvement. Thus, in this model both social and state actors have some room for maneuver, while in the two previous approaches to governance the latitude is almost entirely in the hands of the state. Further, the involvement of social actors is an important component of the legitimation of the state, so that it may have to make some concessions in order to generate sufficient social involvement in decision making. Further, political parties have a greater role to play here than in the previous models. In the state-centric case, competitive parties rather than hegemonic parties are central actors, so that the parties may be involved in brokering relationships between state and society in more open and participative manners than in the previous models.

As noted earlier, "softer" versions of this model are becoming, if anything, more prominent than the corporatist models. The constellation of actors is much the same, and the legitimate rights of participation for the social groups are also the same. What tends to vary is the degree of constraint on the range of social actors, and the openness to a range of interests. Further, although state and society may be linked intimately, there is not the formalistic and hierarchical relationship that is implied in many models of corporatism, such as that of Schmitter (1974).

Processes

Given the above discussion of the actors involved, there are some rather obvious implications for the governance process in these countries. Again, we are moving away from total domination of the process by the state, although the state continues to play a crucial role. The process in this model may appear somewhat more democratic, but still reflects the capacity of the state to manipulate, if not totally control, access to the process.

Goal selection.   This aspect of the policy process remains very much in the hands of the state. We have been arguing, here and elsewhere (Peters, 2000a; Pierre and Peters, 2000), that perhaps the principal role for the state in governance—in almost any conception of the term—is goal selection. Goal selection is an inherently collective action, given that it involves choosing general directions for the society and then moving on to determine the means of reaching those goals. Therefore, it may not be surprising in the least that the state maintains a central, and largely autonomous, position in this part of the process. Societal actors may have input into the process of goal selection, but the decisions are primarily those of the state. After that, the state may have numerous interactions with social actors, primarily over the means to reach those goals.

Decision making.   The manner in which the decision-making stage of the governance process takes place may depend upon which conception of involving societal interests is being practiced. On the one hand, the restrictive version of corporatism outlined by Schmitter (1974) involves state actors dominating and setting the agenda for themselves and the other actors involved. That agenda must then be settled through some bargaining process or another. The more open corporate pluralism characteristic of the Scandinavian countries may permit more bargaining among the actors, although even here the discussions are more likely to be confined to the means for achieving goals rather than the goals themselves. Further, given that a greater number of actors are involved in this version of governance, decision making is likely to be relatively slow, especially when there are consensual norms as in the Scandinavian countries.

Resource mobilization.   Governance systems such as this are largely distributive. As we argued concerning the liberal-democratic approach, this style of decision making is largely distributive. The state is segmented here as it was in the liberal-democratic model, and organizations may be closely linked with particular interests with which they are in corporatist relationships. In this type of distributive system the costs of the public sector (financial and otherwise) may be displaced onto the nonparticipants in the process.

Instruments/implementation.   Policy formulation and policy implementation in this governance model could be described as an interactive process between the state and organized interests. Policy implementation frequently takes on a negotiated nature—not least among interest groups—which means that coercive instruments are less common in this model compared to the previous ones. Organized interests frequently play key roles in the implementation of public policy; indeed, policy implementation sometimes becomes a matter of negotiation between interest organizations. Compared to the previous models, the state-centric model features a state which is more inclined to listen to organized interests. Organized interests are often coopted at the implementation stage, playing an important role in the street-level implementation of public policy. Interest organizations tend to take on these roles rather happily as they are implementing a policy that they had considerable input on, earlier on in the policy process. Thus, if the initial stages of the policy-making process can be rather slow, the later stages tend to be highly efficient because whatever disagreement could have existed between the state and organized interests was resolved early in the process.

Feedback. The state-centric governance model generates better feedback than the first two models largely because of the larger number of points of contact with society and the more elaborate and institutionalized exchanges with key actors in the state's external environment. These exchanges, however, may generate biased feedback; organized interests are, after all, organized *interests* and have a stake in giving feedback which induces the state to direct financial and other resources their way. This means that we should expect to see some degree of competition among interest organizations in providing feedback to the state.

Outcomes

What policy outcomes does the state-centric governance model tend to produce? The answer hinges on how we understand the particular form of state–society relationship which this model displays. The state, we believe, is contingent on—and constrained by—the powerful organized interests that are a defining feature of the political milieu of the state-centric model. But whatever influence these organizations have on public policy is influence granted by the state rather than they have acquired. Thus, the state retains considerable power bases and can, if and when it so chooses, alter the rules of the political game. Also, there is for the most part an understanding among the organized interests that there exists an important distinction between civil society and the state which must be upheld in order not to confuse sectoral political pressures with the integrity of political institutions.

Coherence.   The state-centric model of governance tends to display better horizontal management than in most systems, particularly the corporate pluralist version. This applies to vertical as well as horizontal coherence, because of the involvement of interest groups within relatively coherent structures. To be sure, coherence is frequently strengthened by the organized interests; these organizations have developed considerable policy expertise over time and, moreover, need to present coherent policy advice in order to be perceived as credible and informed actors.

Inclusiveness.   The degree of inclusiveness in this model is intriguing in many ways. On the one hand, this model, everything else being equal, is clearly more inclusive than the étatiste model since it allows for, and encourages, interest group involvement in policy formulation and execution. On the other hand, this inclusion is both selective and indirect; selective because the state can favor some interest organizations more than others and indirect since the inclusion refers more to a limited number of peak organizations which, in turn, are representatives of a larger political constituency. Thus we can say that we have a situation in which Schmitter's state-centric model of corporatism stands against Rokkan's society-centric model of mass political inclusion as "corporate pluralism" (Rokkan, 1966; Schmitter, 1974).

From the point of view of the interest groups, there is a trade-off between inclusion and autonomy. It is extremely difficult for these groups to demand input in various stages of the policy process while at the same time sustaining their autonomy vis-à-vis the state. Thus, this approach to governance tends to coopt segments of society, at once gaining access for the groups and greater acquiescence by society for the state (Heisler, 1974). Having taken part in decisions it becomes difficult for groups to later oppose the decisions of the government, so implementation becomes eased substantially by the cooptation.

Adaptability.   Corporatism as a governance model has a significant drawback in terms of its adaptability; while it is good at distributing gains, it performs much worse when it comes to distributing losses. Adaptability nearly always means altering the distributive patterns of public policy and for most interest groups such changes can only be interpreted as a failure. The biggest adaptation challenge currently facing the state is responding to globalization. Space forbids a closer examination of the state–globalization problematic, but it seems clear that interest groups in state-centric governance need to address this issue almost as much as the state because of the close linkages between state and interests. So far, transnational coordination of interest group activities has been rather limited but this governance model may be a means of coping with challenges related to globalization (Weiss, 1998).

Accountability.   This aspect of the state-centric governance model is often presented as its weakest spot since it tends to separate influence and accountability. Organized interests are perceived as the winners in the political game since they, often successfully, can influence state decisions without having to assume any political responsibility for those decisions and actions. The result is confusion between actors who should be held accountable and those that actually are. This account of the model is slightly exaggerated and incomplete. That elected officials will be held to account gives them considerable clout in fending off political pressures from interest groups. Stated slightly differently, elected officials have an interest in only allowing political pressures that reinforce their own position on the issues. When that strategy is successful, the political elite has coopted interest groups into the policy process and is likely to enjoy support from the rank-and-file membership of those organizations. Meanwhile, the state comes out both large in terms of its governing capacity and enjoying considerable legitimacy as the centerpiece of the governance system. Furthermore, it is sometimes forgotten that the organizations themselves have some internal accountability system which should warrant at least some degree of control on the organizational leadership.

Summary

The state-centric governance model is derived from a set of overarching values which accord both the state and civil society distinct roles in

political life. These values stress participation, proportional representation, inclusion, and transparency. The outcome of this value system
is that the state is thought of as embedded in a society characterized
by a strong civil society. Thus, the state-centric governance model
sees the state as the key actor making priorities and defining objectives and goals, but it does so to considerable extent through an institutionalized exchange with organized interests. This is a model of
policy implementation which we tend to think of as typical to the
Scandinavian countries. However, we can see very similar types of
processes in a country like Japan (Krauss and Pierre, 1993; Pempel
and Tsunekawa, 1979).

The state-centric governance model has many features which we
associate with effective governance, such as a strong, insulated center
combined with institutionalized systems of exchange with the external
environment of the state. It is probably true that much of the positive
developments which characterized those national contexts where this
model is a valid abstraction of the governance processes can be attrib-
uted to these features. It is less clear whether these very features also
explain, to some degree, these countries' problems in adapting to the
changing economy from the mid-1970s onward (Pierre and Peters,
2000). It is difficult not to see the relative weakening of the corporatist
arrangements of interest representation as an institutional change
implemented in order to make the state more apt in responding to
those powerful external changes.

The Dutch governance school

The fourth governance model that we present is in some ways the
most thoroughly researched model, so much so that it makes some
sense to see it perhaps more as an aggregate of a specific governance
research tradition than a model which summarizes governance in a
particular national context. The Dutch governance school is clearly
inspired by Dutch politics and society but has a wider empirical reference. It, to some extent, can be seen as an extension of earlier
research on corporatism and corporate pluralism, so that it can be
seen as applying, to some extent, to the smaller European democracies
with tendencies to have governed by building consensus.

This model of governance accords the state a weaker role than in
the previous models; state decisions and actions reflect interests of
other societal actors to a greater extent, and the institutions of the

state are less insulated from external pressures. Also, decisions are assumed to be more contingent on support from external actors in both policy formulation and especially for implementation. That having been said, the state still operates at a higher political and institutional level than the external actors upon which it depends. While networks and public/private partnerships are defining features of this governance model, the state is the undisputed center of those networks. The key concept in understanding the role of the state in this governance model is that of "steering" and the state—in an often quoted phrase—is said to be "steering at a distance" (Kickert, 1997). Another way of describing this role of the state is that the primary function of the state in this governance model is that it establishes priorities and defines goals and then mobilizes resources from a wide variety of sources, often blending public and private action, to pursue those goals.

Actors

The cast of actors in this governance model could include almost any actor of any societal significance. Local authorities, private businesses, and interest groups all control different types of resources that are attractive to the state. As is the case in network formation, the diversity of actors involved can often be an asset rather than a liability since it broadens the potential domain of the network.

Processes

In the Dutch school of governance, formal decision making is in many ways less important than in the previous governance models. Although the authority of the state is a factor of some significance in this model, primarily in goal formulation, much of the real decisions are made among members of network or partnerships in a rather informal way.

Goal selection. This role remains overwhelmingly a state responsibility. Once the goals have been formulated, the state "steers" and coordinates action toward the goals, albeit at a distance as already noted. Thus, goal selection is conducted at the political level, leaving the decisions on how those goals are best attained to the lower, operative levels. The state retains substantial powers to monitor goal achievement and to reformulate policy when the goals are not being reached by this rather remote form of implementation.

Decision making.   The governance process described by our Dutch colleagues is not very formalized. Stated slightly differently, many of the decisions made by political institutions tend to confirm effective decisions made elsewhere, or, alternatively, are "frame" decisions that give substantive discretion to the operative level. However, the one area where political institutions remain the leading governance agent is in goal formulation.

Resource mobilization.   The Dutch governance model implies a strong capacity for resource mobilization by both state and society. Governance draws on a mixture of public and private resources and organizational capacities. There appears to be an assumption that the cooperation of the two sets of actors will produce considerable leverage and synergy.

Instruments/implementation.   There is no clear distinction between decision making and implementation in the Dutch model as the operative level often tends to function within the fairly wide goals defined by elected officials. It may be that much as argued normatively in the "bottom-up" approach to implementation, goals may be derived from the operational level. There tend to be cooperative arrangements for implementation, involving both sets of actors in the self-regulating networks that are so central to this conception of governance. One of the virtues of this idea is that formulation and implementation can be so closely linked, thereby tending to improve the quality of each. In addition, the range of instruments employed to reach the goals tends to be broader than assumed under the more state-centered approaches, thereby also enhancing the probability of achieving success, and perhaps also reducing the direct costs of implementation to the taxpayers.

Feedback.   Feedback could be slightly problematic in this governance model. If "steering" occurs at a distance, then feedback has a considerable distance to cover, too. Furthermore, network members from the private sector have few incentives to provide feedback to political institutions, especially if that feedback might in any way damage their policy preferences and their position within the network. Thus, the social linkages that should be a strong part of this model may not be so efficacious as assumed. In addition, the relatively low degree of continuity at the operative level can easily become a problem in providing feedback; not only is government threatened with a memory loss, the problem may actually be more acute in society.

Outcomes

The Dutch school of governance is heralded as being efficient in mobilizing resources and generating consent. There is also a strong interest in developing the art of governance, that is, in developing a system of governance that conforms to the society for which it is being used. The typical outcomes of this model of governance are characterized by a fairly high degree of goal attainment, although not without a number of significant problems of narrowly defined goals and limited involvement of many segments of society.

Coherence. The heterogeneity and diversity of the actors involved in this governance model obviously increase the need for coordination. However, coherence remains slightly problematic here; while we should expect a high degree of coordination at the level of individual projects and policy sector, creating coherence across an entire policy sector or among sectors becomes difficult given the fairly weak center. There are some alternative networks, for example, the senior civil service, within government itself that may help to overcome some of the inherent coherence problems of this model, but this should be expected to be a major deficiency in this approach to governance.

Inclusiveness. There is a high degree of (self-proclaimed) inclusiveness in this governance model; indeed, inclusiveness is so high that it—together with a weak center—potentially jeopardizes coherence. That having been said, the system may not be inclusive of groups that are not well organized or that are not accepted as members of the relevant networks. Thus, agricultural networks may not accept alternative views of agriculture (e.g., organic farming) so that there may well be groups who are in fact excluded from the process.

Adaptability. The Dutch school of governance suggests that policy is sometimes implemented by ad hoc, matrix-type task forces with limited organizational continuity. If that should be a more general feature of this governance school, adaptability will not become a problem as there is high organizational flexibility at the operative level but substantial continuity at the senior level of the organizations. There may be less adaptability at other stages of the process, with more limited capacity to reflect changes in the nature of the environment. Networks like other social structures may be conservative and may not readily accept new members.

Accountability.   "Steering at a distance" is a governance style which guarantees the center a key role in the definition of goals and priorities. However, it raises several questions about accountability. Can those who "steer at a distance" be held accountable for the ways in which policy is implemented or for the outcomes of the policy? We noted earlier that the state will also retain some monitoring capacity and part of the governing apparatus of these governments is rather strong, and indeed is now strengthening because of the ideas of New Public Management (NPM) (Pollitt and Bouckaert, 2000). Therefore, accountability may be driven to an increasing extent by performance management and other institutionalized means of accountability; accountability may also be at a distance but there certainly can be accountability.

Summary

One of the more intriguing questions concerning this governance model is to what extent efficiency is explained by the legacy of previously strong institutions (especially for the Netherlands itself). The Dutch school of governance assumes a high degree of organizational capacity in the public sector which it is not particularly committed to sustaining; operating through ad hoc-type of organizations undercuts policy capacity in the longer term. That having been said, the state remains something of an *eminence grise* for the entire process of governance. Further, the Dutch model appears to be directed at using the state sector and its legitimacy, rather than eschewing or totally supplanting it as is the foundation of the next alternative model.

"Governance without government"

The last of the five models of governance is "governance without government." As the label suggests, this governance model accords the least significance to political institutions. The defining feature of this model is the notion that governance is conducted through "inter-organizational, self-governing networks" (Rhodes, 1997). This school thus argues that governance—frequently defined at the level of the policy sector—is organized in an informal fashion among the leading players in the sector and governmental institutions may or may not be part of the governance network. Governance is conceptualized as being "bigger than government" or a more encompassing process than the policy process, and also as a process which sees political and other actors connected in networks. The key argument of this model is that governance occurs largely independently of government and that, indeed, networks with little or no government inclusion can and do control policy sectors. In the more extreme views, these networks are believed to be sufficiently cohesive and omnipotent that they can obstruct the implementation of government policy in their sector if they so choose (Marsh and Rhodes, 1992). There is also an implicit normative argument that this style of governing is superior to the hierarchies of government because it involves the interested parties directly and can be more open and democratic.

Actors

The "governance without government" model makes no prejudgments about the actors involved in governance, with one important exception. The role of government is believed to be quite insignificant and to the extent that political institutions are involved in the governance network they do not enjoy a privileged status. Furthermore, the kind of political institutions that tend to participate in the networks are typically agencies and quangos, both of which operate at considerable distance from elected officials and the representative structures of government. Key participants in the networks are those who play a predominant role in any given policy sector, such as different forms of organized interests, lobbyists, individual public officials from either parliamentary committees or ministries, regional and local government representatives, and so on.

Processes

Overall, the governance process in this model is highly informal and takes place primarily within the networks. Because of the focus on those networks there is little consideration of the difficulties in managing horizontally across multiple networks that may be necessary for effective governance taken in a more general sense.

Goal selection.   The goal selection in this model is characterized more by what is in the interest of the network participants than the broader, collective interests. Networks are to a large extent defined by a commonality of interests—defending the sector from budgetary cutbacks, increasing (if possible) public spending in the sector and governing the sector in such a way that it promotes the visions and interests of the network members—hence goal selection becomes not a very complicated process.

Decision making.   Decision making in these informal networks tends to occur through a consensual model of decision making. The overall political strength of the network depends to a large extent on its internal cohesion, hence there are strong disincentives for any individual member to pursue a narrowly defined selfish objective. We should therefore expect decision making in this model to be informal, swift, and consensual, with sanctions for members of the network which do not conform to collective norms of the structure.

Resource mobilization.   Most of the resources mobilized in this governance model do not come from the actors themselves but primarily from the state. Additionally, the networks can seek to mobilize resources from the network itself, provided the policies reflect the interests of the network. Again, resources must be considered rather broadly to include legitimacy as well as financial resources. Still, paradoxically, the role of the state is denigrated in this approach although the state is expected to be the cash cow that subsidizes the operation of the system.

Instruments/implementation.   Networks are usually excellent structures for policy implementation and governance networks should be expected to be even more so, given that its actors have a strong input on the decisions to be implemented. Thus, the networks will not be called on to implement programs over which they have not had any real control. Observed from the vantage point of the state, however, we obtain a very different picture of implementation through these network structures. As mentioned earlier, studies on sectoral policy networks in the United Kingdom (UK) suggest that these networks are sufficiently strong to, if they so choose, obstruct or delay public policy implementation. Thus, networks are very good at implementing their own ideas and views but can be a formidable obstacle to the implementation of public policy if they believe these policies not to be in the interest of the network. The coordinative and consensual elements of governance in the Dutch system do make this type of obstruction less likely.

Feedback. In theory, this governance model should be equipped to provide accurate and detailed feedback to policy makers. However, given the rivalry that exists between the networks and the structures of government for control over the policy sector, network members have little incentives to provide such feedback. If anything, their feedback is likely to be biased in favor of the interests of the network.

Outcomes

The outcomes of "governing without government" can be assessed at two levels; that of the policy sector and that of the polity. This governance model could be assumed to generate effective governance from the perspective of the networks supposedly controlling the policy sector. What the assessment at this level of analysis overlooks, however, is that policy sectors are at the heart of the state and the collective interest and that sectoral intervention by networks calls into question the linkage between authority and accountability which is the keystone of liberal-democratic theory. Thus efficiency is to some extent attained at the expense of democracy.

Coherence. Again, we must assess the "governance without government" model on two levels. The governance of individual sectors could well be assumed to be reasonably coherent as this is in the interest of the network. However, policy coherence across sectors is poor because of the weak center of government and its lack of a capability to bring together networks that may govern effectively within their own domains. The result in the longer term is therefore fragmentation (what was once called "sectorization") of the state. Further, if we return to the ideas about governance advanced at the outset of this chapter this absence of coherence in goal setting and implementation may present a real barrier to effective governance.

Inclusiveness.   This governance model is not inclusive, despite its initial appearances and some claims about its democratic character. Access to networks is often highly restrictive and may be based on to what extent candidate members share the dominant values of the network. In other cases, the knowledge base of membership in the networks—professional and expert—may inhibit inclusiveness. This lack of inclusiveness, in turn, means that we are not very likely to witness fundamental debates within the networks about proper modes of action; given that access to the network is predicated on your sharing the views of the network.

Adaptability.   Networks can be efficient vehicles to ensure adaptability, provided they have an interest in serving in that capacity. Networks with a significant political component which infuses collective objectives into the network's priorities are in many ways ideal structures to give feedback which is a prerequisite for adaptability. But that is not the type of networks we see in this governance model; here, networks are held together by shared goals and objectives which may or may not coincide with broader political objectives. Thus, adaptability at the level of the state could well be assumed to be impaired by these networks.

Accountability.   As was argued earlier concerning the Dutch school of governance, networks and accountability do not go very well together. It has been suggested that governance—especially a model of governance drawing on a NPM-style model of public service delivery—replaces traditional processes of accountability with new ones such as stakeholderism and customer choice. That may have some relevance to the "governance without government" model of governance, at least in sectors characterized largely by service delivery. However, in most other sectors, political accountability is confused, the effective decision makers are shielded from scrutiny and assessment which instead is directed at elected officials with limited control over different policy sectors.

Summary

"Governance without government" has gained interest among academics and practitioners, to some extent, because it is believed to offer a palatable alternative to "government" as a shorthand for traditional, "old fashioned," hierarchical government that seemingly had lost the confidence of the public. Upon closer inspection, however, this governance model raises several normative concerns regarding democratic input and control, as well as more empirical questions about its capacity to pursue the collective interest of society. True, this statement might be seen as conflating the normative and empirical aspects of the model, but since the advocates of the model sometimes also see "governance without government" as a desirable alternative to the existing order, the debate needs to be conducted at both the empirical and normative levels. At the empirical level, there must also be some question about the extent to which formal government institutions have really been moved so far out of the process of governing, or whether they have merely altered the instruments through which governing is accomplished (Salamon, 2001).

"Governance without government" represents governance carried on with what appears to be relatively little consideration of conventional politics, or of collective interests. If anything, sectoral networks attempt to fend off consideration of those collective interests in order to pursue the objectives of the network itself. This is a model which offers reasonable coherence and adaptability at the level of the individual policy sector, but it does so at the expense of coherence, accountability, and adaptability at the level of the state as a whole. Like all the models of governance discussed here, this one involves making significant trade-offs among values, with the choice of which types of trades to make being to some extent a function of different social and political values.

Concluding comments

The five models are, as we have pointed out, in essence ideal types although there are certainly some cases in the "real world" that do approximate these models very closely. The five models can be seen to be arrayed along an underlying dimension of the direct involvement of the state in the governance process, or conversely a dimension of the role accorded to societal actors in the governing process. We do believe that these five models demonstrate a good deal about the manner in which governance can be arranged within different social and political contexts. They also demonstrate the consequences, for producing effective steering for society, of choosing that these different arrangements can have.

This discussion also leads to a more general argument about the governance capacity of different systemic arrangements involving state and society. The continuum we describe can also be utilized as a means of arraying the governance capacities of these systems, although the pattern is not linear. We argue that there is a nonlinear relationship between societal involvement in governing and governance capacity, with the two ends of the continuum having less governing capacity than the systems toward the middle of the distribution. Rather than the single variable involved in constructing the initial array, here there are two variables. The first is the *authority* of the state, meaning here the capacity of the state to make and enforce binding decisions on the society, and to do so without significant involvement of, or competition from, societal actors. This variable is clearly at its highest level in the étatiste model and gradually wanes as we move along the continuum of the five models.

The second variable that we are considering is the *information* gathering and processing capacity of the state. For this variable, we assume that states must be open to a wide range of information, including much that is uncomfortable and dissonant, if it is to be successful in governing. In other words, the state must be in close contact with the society and utilize social information openly and accurately when governing. This further implies that the state is likely to be in close communication with societal actors who possess much of the information that would be required for effective governing, and also generally that the state must be willing to engage in a formal or informal exchange of power over decisions for that information. The openness of the governance process to multiple sources of information is necessary for the ability to assess alternative strategies and to verify the accuracy of information that may be coming from a single source.

These two variables defining governance capacities appear inversely correlated within the five models of governance we have developed. For example, the étatiste model ranks very high on the first variable of authority, but lacks connection with society. This combination makes it a powerful, but often blind, governor. The state in this model can stumble around, using its great powers without the effects intended because it has such limited and biased information upon which to base decisions. On the other hand, the "governance without government" conception of governing is information rich but lacks the legitimate authority to make effective decisions, especially decisions that apply across the range of society. Thus, the summation of these two attributes is roughly parabolic, with the highest governance capacity appearing in the state-centric model, combining a relatively high level of decisional capability with relatively rich sources of social intelligence.

This representation of the joint governance capacity predicted by these two variables assumes that their interaction is multiplicative, and that they are of relatively equal weight. If their interaction were additive, the net governance capacity would be roughly equal throughout the distribution of the two variables, although the style of governing might be quite different. Therefore, the argument is that both of these variables are necessary, but neither is sufficient, for effective governance. This is, in turn, related to even more fundamental assumptions that governance is about societal steering and therefore involves both detectors and effectors (see Hood, 1986). That is, effective steering systems must be able both to detect environmental conditions and to effect changes in those environmental conditions.

Stated in more concrete terms, this arrangement of the models of governance along this curve would appear to argue that the corporatist, state-centered approach to governing characteristic of much of Continental Europe (and to some extent Scandinavia) should be the most effective form of governance. It is capable of detecting social conditions that may require a policy "fix" and also in putting the policies selected for the fix into effect when decided that they are required. This model represents an apparently effective convergence of public sector abilities to collect information from the surrounding society (often using elements of the society for that purpose) and its capacity to make decisions and put those decisions into effect.

We should stress that this is a very preliminary hypothesis, rather than a definitive statement about governance capacities of states, but it does help to organize the literature on governance. As yet it is based more on theoretical musings rather than on firm empirical evidence. That having been said, however, some evidence that is available does point to the strong governance capabilities of the real-world examples of this model. For example, in a major study of policy success and failure (Bovens *et al.*, 2001) the authors found that the more étatiste

states—France and Spain—in the collection of the six countries ana-
lyzed were in general less successful in governing than were those
countries that permitted a greater role of societal interests. Likewise,
the major example of a liberal-democratic state in that study (the UK)
did not perform as well as the three more corporatist or corporate pluralist regimes—Sweden, the Netherlands, and Germany.

We should also consider implementation more fully when assessing
governance capacity. We have included implementation as one stage
when describing the policy process, but the ability to utilize social
actors to implement policies may be an additional element of the
authority dimension of governance. That is, the étatiste conception
assumes that governments must be responsible for the implementation of their own programs, and therefore also will minimize private
sector implementation of public programs. The capacity to use private
actors for implementation may not only save money for the public
sector, but it may also enhance the legitimacy and effectiveness of
those programs.

It should be clear at this point that this set of conclusions is as
much a research agenda as a summation of what has been written in
the bulk of the chapter. We do believe that these five models capture
a good deal about the way in which governance is now conducted in
many countries of the world. We also believe that it is crucial to move
from those descriptive treatments of governance to a more analytic
approach in which we might begin to assess the role that different
underlying variables in governance play in explaining the relative
success and failure of systems. Thus, we need to think more carefully
about the ways in which we might be able to measure governance
capacity as a concept and then compare the abilities of real governments to govern. Subsequent chapters elaborate these and other
issues in governance research.

3
Governance: A Garbage Can Perspective

Governance is a very old concept, and an even older reality. Societies have always required some form of collective steering and management. Variations in the political and economic order have produced different answers to the fundamental questions about how to provide that steering for society, and how to cope with the range of challenges arising from the society, but some answer has been required, and continues to be required. Governance is not a constant, but rather tends to change as needs and values change. The usual answer to the questions has been the state, but solutions that have been effective, and popular with the public, at one point in time may rather quickly become both ineffective and politically unpopular, and governing represents continuing adaptations of political and administrative activities to changes in the environment, not least of which are changes in the ideas of what constitutes appropriate modes of developing and implementing collective goals.[1]

This chapter addresses adaptation in governance arrangements, and attempts to come to grips with the endemic problems of complexity and uncertainty in governing. The answer provided here, if indeed it is an answer, may be somewhat unsatisfying because it is focused on the indeterminacy of governance in a world without those guiding assumptions. The approach that will be developed, however, may reflect the reality of governance better than more deterministic models based on pure rationality of actors, or on the benign nature of networks. Further, adopting such an unstructured approach does not mean that decisions are not made, and we argue that decisions are made but not always in the open and in participative ways as is implied by some of the literature on changes in governance.

The shifts in styles of governance involve shifts in the instruments used for governing as well as the content of governing. Shifts in the content and goals of governance are the more obvious features of the transformations. This change in solutions to the basic questions of the political economy was obvious during the 1980s and 1990s as most countries of West Europe adopted neoliberal ideas of the role of the state, and reduced the role of the public sector significantly (Campbell and Pedersen, 2001). The transformations of the goals of governing in Eastern Europe and some countries in the Third World, driven in part by international organizations and other donors, were even more dramatic. Likewise, the welfare state continues to be redefined as neoliberal ideas shape the manner in which governments manage social problems of inequality and provide income for people over the life cycle (Pierson, 1994).

No matter what the overall goals and content of governing may be, there are a range of instruments available to achieve the goals. The instruments literature (Peters and Van Nispen, 1998; Salamon, 2002) coming from public administration and public policy has concentrated on understanding these "tools" at the level of the individual tool. That is, how does a loan guarantee differ from a voucher as a means of putting a program into effect? At a more general level, however, changes in governing have tended to entail movements away from authority-based instruments and to involve governments working through less intrusive means. In the terminology developed by Hood (1986), there has been a shift away from authority based on instruments in favor of instruments based on treasure and nodality (information).

The movement away from authority-based instruments and ruling through those conventional mechanisms of social control has occurred in large part because of changes occurring within government itself, and perhaps more importantly because of changes in public reactions to the actions of the public sector. There is by now a significant literature documenting declining public confidence in government institutions and in the politicians who populate them (Dogan, 1999; Norris, 1996). This decline in public confidence in government has been most pronounced in the United States (US) (Bok, 1997) but it has been observed even in countries with a long history of benign and effective government (Holmberg and Weibull, 1998; Ministry of Finance, 1998). With the decline in confidence in government, the capacity to achieve goals through instruments that depend upon authority, and therefore on legitimacy, is diminished as Woodside (1998) has stressed the importance of less intrusive means of governing for some time, but that point is now being forced upon governments.

The garbage can model

Although there has been a good deal of thinking and writing about governance, the term remains largely descriptive rather than explanatory. This descriptive nature of a great deal of the governance literature reflects in part its attempt to capture virtually the entirety of the policy process, becoming something of a later day systems analysis of politics. To the extent that the term is used less generally, the concept often relies upon network thinking, and is hampered by the absence of mechanisms of conflict resolution and decision making in that body of theory. Politics is about contradictory and conflicting interests and the argument that social networks are capable of governing is contingent upon their capacity to resolve those differences.

Whatever approach one may take to governance, save the most étatiste (see earlier), the very use of the term governance represents an acceptance of some movement away from the conventional authority-based style of governing. That movement is in favor of approaches to governing that rely less on formal authority and more on the interaction of state and societal actors. Further, the questioning of state authority and capacity implied in the use of governance means that some of the rationalist perspectives on the role of governments in governing may also be brought into question.[2] The "new governance" literature stresses networks, bargaining, and interaction rather than hierarchies as the best way to govern, and the best way to understand governance. Thus, this literature contains both normative and empirical dimensions.

One way to move from a strictly descriptive sense of governance is to employ the garbage can model of decision making developed by Cohen *et al.* (1972) as a means of exploring the ways in which governance can be supplied in a world that is less clearly governed through authority. Based, not surprisingly, on the management of universities (see also March and Olsen, 1976), the garbage can model rejected conventional linear models of decision making in favor of a less determinate and less rational (in the usual interpretation of that word) forms of making decisions. The fundamental assumption driving this model is that, rather than being programmed or pre-dictable, decisions in many situations are more the result of the confluence of opportunities, individuals and ideas (see later).

The garbage can was developed as a means of examining the behav-ior of organizations, but its authors discussed its being applied to "decision situations" as well as to organizations per se. Further, at least one of its authors of the original article has discussed the possi-bility of its application to the EU as a rather diffuse political system (Olsen, 2001).[3] Likewise, Christopher Hood (1999) examined the relationship of this model to governing more generally, focusing on the relationship to the impact of unstructured situations to risk and regulation. The model appears to have some utility for understanding decision situations that are broader than individual organizations, and may well be applicable to situations in which organizations themselves are the principal players. We argue that in these broader settings organizations may be the most reintegrated and decisive actors in anarchic decision situations and therefore will have some advantages in producing actions that conform to their preferences.

The garbage can model of organizational decision making is one link in an extended chain of intellectual development in organiza-tional theory that is described as "bounded rationality," and is founded upon the insights of Herbert Simon and other members of the so-called Carnegie School of decision making (1947; Cyert and March, 1963; March and Simon, 1957; see Bauer and Gergen, 1968). Simon famously argued that the demands of full-blown rationality were too great for any individual or organization to be able to achieve when making decisions. Therefore, organizations are best understood as acting rationally only within narrowed boundaries, with their rational action range being determined by their own routines, norms, technologies, and interests. Thus, Simon's familiar term of satisficing can be used to describe behavior that seeks outcomes that are "good enough" rather than comprehensively utility maximizing. This crite-rion of rationality should not be seen, however, as excessively minimalist, given that finding policy solutions that are "good enough" can itself be extremely demanding, and rational from the perspective of minimizing decision-making costs rather than maximizing the utility of the outcomes produced.

Bryan Jones (2001) has further developed the concept of bounded rationality in the context of governing and policy making. Jones was interested in the capacity of organizations to adapt to changes in their environment. Institutions tend to develop routines and rules of thumb that enable them to perform well at one point in time but also result in slow adaptation. In governance terms this argument is analogous to the historical institutionalist perspective of path dependency and the means through which existing patterns of policy are maintained. The garbage can model provides an explanation of how adaptations can take place even in the absence of full information and the other conditions that are necessary for comprehensive rationality to be implemented.

As we apply the garbage can model to governance we argue that this model is capable of being used to understand governance in the political environment. In particular, given that the capacity of authoritative actors to structure decisions has been diminished and that even many structured modes of political participation have been weakened, the garbage can model seems to be more applicable. With those changes both the inputs into politics and the processes by which decisions are reached are less predictable, and less likely to be effective on a regular basis. The outcomes of the policy process may represent the confluence of streams of possibilities rather than a rational search for the best option. This model of governing is by itself not predictive, but it does provide a useful means for interpreting many changes in contemporary governance.

Organized anarchies

The garbage can model grew out of the general concern with bounded rationality within organizations, and other decision-making situations, in which linear and fully rational modes of choice would be unlikely if not completely impossible. Although Bendor *et al.* (2001: 174) find reasons to distinguish the garbage can model from the remainder of the bounded rationality literature, there does appear to be a strong family resemblance, if not a direct parental connection, among these approaches to organizations and decision making. If nothing else the garbage can model and bounded rationality both reject fundamentally rationalist perspectives, and seek alternative means of understanding how institutions are able to muddle through in complex and poorly defined decision situations. As for the organized anarchies that are central to the garbage can, three features characterize these organizations or situations:

(1) *Problematic preferences.* In a setting such as that assumed to exist within an organized anarchy, it is difficult to impute the consistency of preferences that are required for standard, rationalistic models of decision making to perform well. Preferences in the garbage can model are inconsistent among the participants and/or ill-defined. Further, preferences may be subject to limited discussion because of the political difficulties that such inconsistency may generate within an organization, or a political system. The point here is that preferences held by individual actors may well be consistent, and could be held quite passionately, but preferences within the decision-making structure as a whole are not consistent.

In an organized anarchy preferences are *discovered* through actions. Note that in this context individual actors (individual or collective) may have consistent preferences, but the policy-making system *qua*-system is assumed to encounter substantial difficulty in reconciling those varied preferences and making them coherent. The shifts characteristic of a post-authority governance make resolving any conflicts all the more difficult. Those difficulties are analogous to those that political scientists have identified with "blocked" policy making or "stalemate" for some time (see, for example, Crozier, 1979), but these blockages may be more severe because of the decline of authority-based instruments for resolving blockages.

To the extent that it can move, the organized anarchy consequently faces the danger of falling into something like a joint decision trap, with decisions being made by the lowest common denominator (Scharpf, 1997). If preferences are discovered for the system as a whole, rather than being imposed, then the only ones available may be minimal movements away from the status quo—the classic incremental solution to policy problems. If there are to be movements away from this minimalist form of governance then intersections with at least one other stream within the garbage can—either individuals as entrepreneurs or opportunities (crises, windfalls, or whatever) may be necessary.

(2) *Unclear technology.* The processes through which organized anarchies are able to survive, and even to prosper, are often poorly understood by the members of those structures. There may be a rather simple trial and error process of learning, and incremental change in the system, but the structuring of the system is done largely by adaptation rather than comprehensive strategic planning from the center. Thus, just as the goals of governing may emerge rather than being imposed from a central "mind of government," so too are the means of achieving those ends also likely to be emergent rather than planned.

This absence of clear and centrally controlled technologies for governing is consistent with a good deal of contemporary discussions about governance. Whereas government might once have had well-known and accepted means of implementing policy and producing the actions that were required, there is now a less clear armamentarium available to would-be governors. The good news in this is that there is a wider range of instruments available for government to use when implementing its programs, many of which involve the use of the private sector. Part of the wide scale reform of government over the past several decades (Peters, 2001a) has been to create means of achieving collective purposes through less direct, partnership methods (Pierre, 1998), or other means involving private and not for profit actors.

As well as a wider range of "technologies" for achieving ends for the public sector, the very lack of clarity in the "garbage can" model of governing may be an advantage for the emergent public sector. While the traditional public sector and its limited range of responses to problems (and opportunities) may have been able to produce results, it did so at some cost, and the lack of clarity that is typical of bounded rationality and its more evolutionary and trial and error style of governing has the potential for political benefits if not necessarily for enhanced effectiveness in governing. This emergent style of more tentative governing may be an antidote to the need of many governments, and many politicians, to claim that they have answers for the problems that confront society. While claiming that solutions to policy problems are not only possible but even readily available may be politically necessary at times, it may not reflect the reality of the knowledge base available to governments in many policy areas. Several decades ago, the economist Richard Nelson (1968) argued that governments did not have the technology to cope with most social problems.[4] Regrettably that conclusion still stands, so that the public sector is often making decisions without a clear understanding of the process into which it is intervening. Given that weakness of the knowledge base available to many decision makers, and the associated uncertainty about policy, recognition of the problem, and a willingness to avoid premature closure of policy options may represent a more "rational" approach to governing than a more self-assured approach.

(3) *Fluid participation.* Members of organized anarchies vary in the amount of time and effort they are prepared to devote to any structure or situation, and indeed membership in such an anarchy may itself be problematic. Thus, the boundaries of the organizations, or the decision situations, are fluid and uncertain, and the decision-process within them tend to be poorly defined. The attempts of any actor to become involved in any decision may be capricious, and certainly cannot be readily predicted, even from prior analogous situations. Given the game-like nature of this process the potential participants never totally ignore the possibilities of involvement; they may choose the degree of involvement depending upon the perceived probabilities of winning, or perhaps on the basis of less utilitarian criteria.

This description of life in an organized anarchy bears some resemblance to discussions of policy making in networked governments. In the conventional state-centric conception of governing, participation in the policy process might be managed in one of several ways. Perhaps the most important principal players would be governmental actors, rather than actors from civil society, and they would be mandated to participate or would find it in their political or organizational interest to participate. To the extent that elements of civil society are involved in the policy process this tends to be organized by the state, rather than being autonomous decisions by those actors themselves. That structuring of participation may be through pluralist selection of a limited number of quasi-official representatives of societal segments, or it may be more corporatist or corporate pluralist in which multiple interests are brought together. These structures are capable of creating more integrated preferences for the society. The segmentation that characterizes much of government can be alleviated.

This characteristic of erratic and uncertain participation does not necessarily mean that there will be less. In fact, it may mean quite the contrary. As state-imposed constraints on participation become more relaxed, there are more demands for involvement, and also for more participation in decisions. Charles Jones (1982) argued some years ago that the "iron triangles" in American politics had been transformed into "big sloppy hexagons," but the geometry of political participation can now be described only by more complex structures. At the same time that societies are presumably becoming more atomistic and less organizational, the level of mobilization around particular issues remains strong, or has perhaps even increased in intensity (Tarrow, 1998). This is certainly political participation, but it is not the conventional versions. It may be that we are not necessarily bowling alone; rather we may simply be bowling in new leagues each week.

This point about shifting forms of participation raises yet another issue concerning the nature of societal participation in this "garbage can model" of governance. The nature and structure of the groups attempting to participate in government are changing in a manner that emphasizes the fluid and uncertain nature of contemporary governance. There is a good deal of evidence that involvement in the range of stable organizations—both interest groups and the traditional political parties—that were deeply embedded in the political process is declining. In their place there are a number of short-lived, and/or single-issue organizations that have begun to attract greater participation. We may speculate about the reasons for the apparent failure of interest groups and parties (Dalton and Wattenberg, 2000), but that they are less capable of channeling participation does appear clear.

The decline in political participation through conventional means rather obviously enhances the fluidity of participation in government and hence some of the predictability of the process. This fluidity affects not only the types of pressures being placed on decision makers but it also affects the political calculations that those decision makers are likely to make about policies. In a less fluid process the decision makers can calculate the likely political consequences of decisions, even if they may be uncertain about the effectiveness of the policies being adopted.[5] This aspect of fluid participation is closely related to the problematic nature of preferences in an organized anarchy. Again, individual actors have preferences and hold them with some intensity, and perhaps with even greater intensity than in more structured situations of decision making, but their multiplicity and the fluidity of participation makes integration across the policy system more difficult than in a more structured system.[6]

A final point about the more uncertain nature of participation in contemporary governments is that more participation appears to be directed at the output side of government rather than at the input side. That is, rather than worrying about attempting to influence the policy decisions made by legislatures or political executives, a greater share of political activity is becoming directed at influencing the behavior of bureaucracies. Further, it is not so only at the top of the bureaucracy, but rather at the lowest levels of the administrative system as well. Members of the public as well as organized interests now find it more useful to limit attempts at exerting influence to local schools, or their own housing projects, or local environmental problems (Sorensen, 1997), rather than acting on a national scale. This may make perfect sense in terms of the capacity to change policies and programs that have direct impacts on the individual, but it also directs the emphasis of policy making on the particular rather than on general policies and their (possible) coherence.

Governing in the garbage can

The above discussion of the nature of organized anarchies at the heart of the garbage can model may well make one pessimistic about the possibilities of governing in a post-authority political system. That pessimism would, of course, be based upon accepting the notion that the garbage can is a reasonable approach to understanding contemporary governance. While we do not argue that this is the only way in which to approach governance in this significantly altered environment, we do argue, as earlier, that it does provide a reasonable and useful window to the process of governing.

The next step in using this approach is to consider the way in which decisions are made in the context of an organized anarchy. The basic argument of the garbage can model, given its anarchic basis, is that decision making is not structured, orderly, and "rational" in the way that might be expected from much of the decision making literature in policy analysis and allied fields (Nurmi, 1998). Rather, decision making in the public sector as seen through the lens of this model reflects the serendipitous, and almost accidental, confluence of streams of problems, solutions, opportunities, and actors. In this view the rationalistic conception of problems searching for solutions and actors pursuing their interests in a purposive manner is replaced by decision making that may be dominated by the appearance of opportunities. As John Kingdon (1995) has argued, "policy windows" open and then policy entrepreneurs must be prepared to exploit the opportunities.

This basic description of policy making in organizational settings has, we argue, parallels in decision making in contemporary political systems. There may have been a heyday of rationalist policy making, but the contemporary world of governance does not appear to be practising it.[7] As faith in government has dropped, the faith in rational planning, forecasting, and other forms of rational decision making has dropped even more rationally. This does not mean that the quest to make "government work better and cost less" has waned, and if anything the reforms of the past several decades indicate quite the opposite. There are continuing attempts to improve government performance, but these depend more upon the use of market or political power to impose greater efficiency and responsiveness, rather than depending upon rational processes to produce optimal answers to policy problems.[8]

Agenda setting is a crucial aspect of policy making in the garbage can model. That is true of all approaches to public policy, but the loose structuring of the organized anarchy, and the absence of dominant institutional drivers in the system means that deciding what issues will be considered is crucial for deciding outcomes. The model of convergent streams and problematic preferences means that issues that might rationally be considered important for governing may be avoided. Avoidance is one of the common outcomes of the computer simulations of decision making in the garbage can, given the absence of coherent preferences and of a mechanism for driving action ahead.

Other studies of management taking the garbage can perspective have found that individual entrepreneurs become the crucial means of producing action. This finding is, of course, true for Kingdon's work on agenda setting in government but research in the private sector and the third-sector organizations also demonstrates that individual involvement and entrepreneurship is crucial to generating action. The centrality of individuals is not only a result of personal power and political skills, it may also be a function of the uncertainty of the situation and the desire of participants to be able to associate proposals for resolving the issue with individuals who advocate them.

Paradoxes in the garbage can

The seemingly irrational and disorderly assumptions characteristic of the garbage can model, and to some extent, much of the "new governance" literature, masks more determinate patterns of policy making that belie the seemingly unstructured, chaotic pattern of making decisions. The loose structuring and seemingly participatory nature of the arrangements within the garbage can hide rather effectively the exercise of power, and the ability of a limited number of actors to shape outcomes. The most fundamental paradox is that a system of governance that is assumed to be open, inclusive, and indeterminate may be more determined by power than are more structured systems. We have already noted that from an agenda-setting perspective, issues that are appropriately formulated, that is they match some of the preconceptions of individuals and organizations charged with making decisions, are more likely to be successful than are less clearly defined issues and ideas. As Heimer and Stinchcombe (1999) have argued, pressing an issue that is not formulated "appropriately" for a decision situation may be dismissed simply as complaining.

The garbage can model may place an even greater emphasis on agenda setting than do other varieties of decision making. Given that the garbage can depends upon a confluence of streams, and the emergence of opportunities for action, one may not expect a great deal of preparation of issues. Much the same can be assumed of networks at the heart of a great deal of thinking about governance. The absence of authority at the heart of this model makes the emergence of issues more uncertain than it might be in more routinized and regulated structures for decision making.

If we consider the remainder of the policy process, some of the same dominance of actors who are well integrated into that process, and who can exercise some form of power within the process, also can be observed. Governance ideas, and especially the garbage can conception of governance being utilized in this chapter, do imply more loosely structured, indeterminate, and uncertain processes of steering society than those characterizing traditional hierarchical forms of governing. However, as at the agenda-setting stage, the policy formulation stage of the process may be dominated by actors who have clear ideas and who are able to put those ideas into operational forms. Perhaps most obviously, bureaucratic organizations are accustomed to translating their conceptions into policies and so are likely to be major players when there are fewer hierarchical constraints.

A significant source of the advantage for more powerful actors is the general absence of legal frameworks within which the garbage can functions. Formal rules, and especially constitutional rules, are mechanisms for ensuring access, and protecting minority rights in the decision-making process. Part of the logic of the garbage can model is that there are few formalized rules governing the interaction of the actors, and the actors themselves make most of the decisions about involvement. Further, the governance literature tends to de-emphasize formal rules in favor of negotiation, networking, and bargaining. Although those terms are neutral and appear benign, the more powerful tend to be most effective in all of these processes, everything else being equal.

Having an answer to the policy problem, and having clear preferences, also tends to favor the more powerful actors in the decision-making process. As noted earlier, the advantage of having clearly defined preferences is enhanced when there are fewer rules and formalized procedures. In such a decision-making system it may not be the societal actors who might have been advantaged by a shift toward a governance model, but rather it may be bureaucracies and other formal institutions that are able to prosper in that setting. Thus, the garbage can may be a natural locus for bureaucratic politics[9] rather than the locus for more open and effective participation by societal actors—the presumed winners in governance. This is, of course, exactly the opposite of the expected outcomes of a model of decision making that appears as loosely structured as does this one.

Another component of the advantage for bureaucracies and other institutional actors in a governance or garbage can situation is control of information. Management scientists who have used the garbage can model to understand organizational processes found that control of information was crucial to controlling decisions (Padgett, 1980).

We should expect bureaucracies to gain a substantial advantage here over societal actors, despite the attempt of those actors to enhance their capacity to provide alternatives to official views of policy, or even the actions of governments to create paid interveners and other information alternatives (see Gormley, 1983). Information is crucial in all decision processes but its power may be enhanced when the process itself is poorly defined, and the problems become defined along with the solutions.

Conclusion

This chapter has been an exploration of whether the concept of the garbage can, developed as a means of understanding behavior in organizations, can be used to understand governance in the contemporary public sector. The principal reason for pursuing this concept is that the apparent decline in the authority of the state in governing has produced some of the same conditions in the public sector as a whole that were presumed to exist in the "organized anarchies" within organizations. We have argued that there are sufficient analogies between these two decision situations to permit using the garbage can with reference to contemporary governance. In particular, the declining level of structure in the manner in which demands are being made on government, and the apparently greater difficulty in making decisions within government, appear to make the analogy with the garbage can viable.

Not only is the analogy between organizational and more comprehensive forms of policy making viable, but it is also useful. By looking at the process of governing as analogous to the garbage can model of organizations, we can begin to understand better the implications of changes in the capacity of governments to impose their programs through authority-based mechanisms. In particular, the uncertainty of technology and the difficulty in making preferences coherent given the increased variety of participants in the process may help to explain the difficulties many governments now encounter when making decisions. Governance is a game that many people and organizations get to play, and that wider participation and some uncertainty about the rules make outcomes less predictable.

Perhaps the most important outcome of this analysis is that the rather benign assumptions of much of the governance literature may disguise some less open and democratic implications of the concept. While governance implies wider participation, the analogy with the garbage can would lead us to expect power to be as important or even more important than in state-centric conceptions of governing. The role of political and institutional power may be especially pronounced when governments are forced to think and act horizontally, and to attempt to create more coherent patterns of governing. That integration across issue domains may be achievable only through the use of some form of power, whether derived from expertise or position. If governing is providing a relatively coherent set of priorities to society, then governance may find that power and authority have not been lessened but only redefined.

4
Governance and Governability: Time, Space, and Structure

Previous chapters have argued that the adaptive capacity of political institutions is an important aspect of governance, particularly the extent to which the state can provide direction, meaning, and coherence in governing. As was suggested in Chapter 1, the process of governing represents a continuing set of adaptations of political and administrative activities to changes in the environment. The principal adaptation has been an increasing involvement of societal actors in governance and with that change some blurring of any clear distinction between the public and private sectors. This statement does not mean that government has abdicated its responsibilities to steer the society, but only that there is now a wider range of instruments available for achieving public purposes (see Salamon, 2001).

The "étatiste" and the "governing without government" models of governance can serve as examples of the breadth of the current governance debate. As well as these alternative stereotypes of governing there is a perspective that to some extent permeates thinking in both camps. This is a fundamental set of assumptions about the linear and rational elements of the process. The sense in much of this literature is that governance proceeds by first identifying and choosing collective goals for the society and then developing the mechanisms for achieving those goals. That is certainly true in the top-down conceptions of the state-centric literature but is also to some extent indwelling in the "governance without government" view. In this alternative conception of governance, networks do within their policy domains what government is meant to do for the society as a whole, and determine the direction of the policy area as well as implement the set of goals that has been selected. Politics does matter, and there are policy failures in both of these conceptions of governing (see Bovens *et al.*, 2001). The very notion of failure, however, assumes some strong sense of goal seeking in the policy process as it grinds along.[1]

Governance is far from being linear in how it operates and there are barriers to that linearity that exist in time, space, and across political structures (most notably networks). Rather than being linear and determinate, the governance process can be conceptualized at least as well as being more than a little chaotic. In that conceptualization, policy outcomes may be structured by accidental events and conjunctures rather than through conscious design. Further, we argue that this rather chaotic conceptualization is more applicable at present than in the (relatively) recent past. Especially as governance has moved away from the hierarchical, institutionally constrained, and state-centric conception, the more disjointed notion of governing is increasingly appropriate and increasingly crucial for understanding what is happening in governance.

The incremental conception of the policy process (Hayes, 1981) is familiar, and to some extent is a function of the internal conflicts within the policy process. The conception of the policy process that we are developing, however, will extend beyond that notion and will not necessarily privilege small deviations from the status quo.[2] Indeed, unlike the incrementalist conception, the view that we advance will be able to account for more radical departures from the prevailing policy regimen. The difficulty is that those deviations may not be in the directions that might have been assumed from attempts to impose order on the process and even from the directions of the apparent political pressures.[3] While the historical institutionalists and the incrementalists can provide a rather predictable conceptual world for policy—perhaps excessively so—we argue that the deinstitutionalization of some aspects of policy making may make the policy world substantially less determinate and predictable.

This apparently chaotic conception of governance generates rather paradoxical outcomes for policy and the conduct of governing. The loosely structured and seemingly incoherent nature of governance that has been argued here and elsewhere to be emerging in most industrialized democracies might appear to be associated with open and democratic outcomes. In reality, however, the outcomes of these loosely structured policy processes are in many ways less open and more structured by political power than is even the state-centric approach that it appears to have replaced.

Governability

Governability is the "flip side" of governance. If there is to be any success at providing collective direction to society, then there must be at least a modicum of willingness to be governed, or at least some degree of insight that governance serves not just the interests of the state but also that of society; the role of government in providing a regulatory structure for the market is a case in point (Kenworthy, 1995; Polanyi, 1942; Schumpeter, 1947). In addition the presence of some organizational capacity within the society to which the governance is being supplied can assist government in providing collective direction. This need for cooperation from society is especially evident as the conventional conceptions of top-down governance become less acceptable, and there is a need to create effective interactions and mingling of the two elements of the governance equation.

It should be noted here that the lessened acceptability for hierarchical governance is found within government itself as well as within the society that it is meant to be governing (see Peters, 2001a). Many of the reforms of governance implemented during the past several decades have replaced hierarchical instruments with more cooperative forms of goal setting and policy implementation. Decentralization, devolution to autonomous and quasi-autonomous organizations, and the growth of partnership arrangements have all diminished the command and control nature of governing in favor of more indirect "new governance" (Salamon, 2002).[4] While failures of some of these formats have produced some reassertion of the direct role of government in the process, it is also fair to say that there have been some lasting transformations. Furthermore, most states in the Western world have taken some pride in presenting themselves as "enabling" states more than commanding and intervening ones. The notion of "steering, not rowing" coined by Osborne and Gaebler (1991) in the context of administrative reform has been diffused to apply to the role of the state in society more generally.

Within the context of the EU the need to blend state and society becomes ever more complicated as there are multiple societies that must be aligned at some minimal level. There is a European society, and there are a set of European networks surrounding policy areas, but those are often poorly coordinated with, or are supplanted by, persisting national networks and patterns of policy (Börzel and Risse, 2002). Further, simply the differences in policy and administrative patterns (Knill, 1998; Van Waarden, 1995) in the countries of the Union may make the argument that a common society exists more tenuous. Given that, supplying governance may be thought to be even more demanding.

Elements of governability

Governability can be conceptualized in the abstract but there are several elements that can be used to illuminate the concept. These dimensions focus not only on the nature of the society that is to be governed, but also, and more importantly, on the linkage of state and society. This discussion is premised on two assumptions. The first is that governance and governability are linked and that to be successful there must be linkage. The second, and related, premise about governance is that different forms of linkage are appropriate for different configurations of states and societies. Some of the concerns about both of the extreme conceptualizations of governing may be functions of attempting to understand patterns of governing outside of the context for which they make sense and are effective.

Confidence in institutions

One of the crucial elements of governability is public confidence in the institutions that are meant to provide governance to the society. The bad news, as has been so widely commented on in both academic and journalistic accounts of contemporary politics, is that this level of confidence and trust has been declining, even in societies that have had a record of benign and effective government (Norris, 1996; Nye *et al.*, 1997). The loss of confidence is a virtual universal phenomenon, with even benign and effective governments, such as those of Scandinavia (Holmberg and Weibull, 1998), suffering virtually the same rates of loss, albeit beginning from a higher level, as have countries such as the US that have had a generally antistatist perspective for some time.

Networks

The somewhat dismissive comments concerning the "governance without government" approach should not be seen as rejecting totally the importance of networks and other mechanisms for connecting state and society in governance. As already noted, we do understand the increased importance of these structures in contemporary governance. That having been said, we do not accept that they can, or should, provide governance to society by themselves. Empirically, networks do not have the capacity to perform many of the tasks required for governance, and especially for democratic governance.[5] In particular, networks are not effective at conflict resolution or in goal setting, assuming that there are any significant differences in ideas among the members of the network.

Further, although networks do have elements of self-referentiality they are not so autonomous from the public sector as some of their advocates might believe. While governments are depicted as rather inept, bumbling entities in many of the accounts of the more extreme network theorists, we argue that states often are an essential element of the network, and in many (if not most) instances actually initiate the formation of the network. Network formation is an attractive policy instrument for the "enabling state" since it provides additional capacity to act with minimal cost. If nothing else public sector organizations provide the targets for the activities of networks, and the justification for their existence. For example, if we conceptualize conventional notions of neo-corporatism as a special case of networks, then the sanctioning by the state is an essential element in the creation and maintenance of the network.

At a more normative level networks probably lack legitimacy to all but their own members, and perhaps lack genuine legitimacy even to many members of those structures. If these arrangements of organizations are, in Eastonian terms, responsible for the authoritative allocation of values for a society, then they require some better developed means of accountability and legitimation. The simplest way to obtain the legitimacy required to govern effectively is to have some direct grant of power from the state. Again one finds that grant of power in various forms of corporatism, not just in the rather stringently defined versions such as that used by Schmitter. In many forms of meso-corporatism and corporate pluralism, perhaps especially those in policy areas such as agriculture and fishing, one finds grants of authority to legally defined social networks.

The linkages generated through networks is one contribution to the governability of society. Rather than having the capacity to govern on their own, networks are better conceptualized as linkages between state and society that may be able to enhance the capacity of each to achieve desired ends. That statement assumes a number of things about networks and about the nature of governance. The first assumption is that the state has desired ends, and the preferred manner of thinking of that phenomenon may be that particular organizations or segments of the state have preferences.[6] If we think of governance as the creation of relatively coherent and coordinated policy preferences within the state, then the network linkages to particular groups may only exacerbate governance problems. Network linkages may further divide political systems that have their own internal divisions. The important point we wish to make is that networks are in no way inconsistent with a style of governance in which the state plays a significant role.

Civil society

Another way of addressing the societal element of governability component is to utilize the now familiar, and perhaps somewhat overused, notions of civil society and social capital (Coleman, 1982; Putnam, 1993). In many ways these concepts must be considered prior to that of networks, given that networks assume the existence of social organizations, and for students of civil society the formation of organizations is in essence the dependent variable. Social capital is not a real problem for the organizationally dense societies of northern Europe, but it is for some Mediterranean members of the EU, and certainly will be for many of the candidate members of the Union.

Even if the analyst is not concerned directly with the role of networks in governing, the social organizations in civil society that might form the basis for networks can still be an important element for governance and governability. Social organizations can perform a variety of functions in the governability equation. They first serve as a means for pressing wishes and demands on government from society. Private sector organizations are also important for implementing public programs. Even more fundamentally, civil society organizations mediate between the state and the individual, making society less atomistic and government more controllable.[7]

Further, if there is a virtuous spiral in the involvement of individuals in social organizations and the formation of trust, then the development of social capital may help to overcome the (increasing) tendency of citizens to regard the actions of their governments with more than a little skepticism. Of course, the creation of trust within social organizations may not be spread so easily to the state as has been assumed by some scholars working in the civil society. If there is not this diffusion of trust to the state then the now popular strand of civil society research to some extent conflicts with the network, and "governance without government" ideas about governance and governability. If one assumes (as some of the more nihilist literature does) that the fundamental logic of governance is (or again perhaps should be) to evade the control of the public sector, then an increase in the capacity for social organization may decrease rather than increase the governability of society.

The above point requires that we consider even more clearly governance as the linkage between state and society rather than the two entities as separate and autonomous social structures operating independently as some strands of theorizing (both state- and network-centric) have assumed. Indeed, the two contending and rather extreme conceptions of governance mentioned earlier are based on assumptions that one "sector" or other is capable of governing almost entirely by itself. We believe that both of those conceptions of governing are inadequate, especially in the context of the increasing importance of the private sector organizations in governing.

Regulation

Finally, we turn to regulation as another means of linking state and society and enhancing governability. It might appear somewhat eccentric to discuss regulation as an aspect of governability, given that it is usually conceptualized as a central activity of the political system itself. Indeed, regulations generally do reflect the institutional logic(s) of state action, and may encounter problems of implementation and effectiveness thereby (Kagan, 2001). This is the root of some of the "governance without government" argument, or is a more moderate version that is characteristic of many Dutch scholars, as discussed in Chapter 2 (Kooiman, 1993; in 't Veld, 1991). Regulations in this view do not match the social reality into which they are being interjected and, therefore, do not produce the intended results.

The logic of linkage for regulation is that the regulations being imposed must, at least over time, conform more to the social and economic reality that they are meant to control. This can be done through the implementation process, and a reverse version of "regulatory creep," or it can be accomplished through political negotiation, or it may be accomplished through the evasion of the regulations by social actors who have the capacity to do so.[8] However it is brought about, the mutual adaptation of state and society around attempts at regulation appears to be a crucial aspect of linkage between the two social sectors.[9] The effectiveness of regulation as a linkage is contingent on two factors. One is the degree to which regulation reflects not just the preferences and desires of state actors but also those of society. Networks in which state actors and societal actors can exchange views on the need for, and the nature of, regulation increase the chances for regulation which is effective, timely, and viewed as appropriate by society. In this perspective then regulation becomes both a cause and effect of the broader linkages that can exist between state and society.

The other factor is time. Regulation is a dynamic linkage between state and society. Regulations that prove to be inefficient or illegitimate tend to be abolished, partly in order to ensure that other existing regulations will not become perceived as equally illegitimate. Similarly, society tends to adapt to new regulations over time, providing that these new rules are considered appropriate. This process of mutual adaptation is sometimes disrupted by "leaps" in societal or economic development. Globalization may be considered such a "leap"; although initiated by states through deregulation of capital and financial markets, globalization created an international economy devoid of any significant regulatory structure. As the impacts of this new economic order have been felt strongly by numerous national governments, there is now a growing debate on how to define and implement a regulatory structure on the global level.

As regulation has faced social and political mobilization against its intrusion into social life there have been a number of institutional changes in the way in which it is practiced. In addition to the use of social actors in the implementation of regulations (May and Winter, 1999) there are a variety of ways of involving the regulated in the construction of the rules they will be obliged to follow, for example, "neg-reg" in the US. These are means of ameliorating some of the political complaints about regulation as well as a means of institutionalizing linkages between the two sets of actors in the process.

Time, space, and organization

The conception of governance that we advance is focused on three dimensions of deviations[10] from the linearity inherent in much of the governance literature, and again especially the state-centric model of governing as we saw in the opening chapters. In the context of the EU the spatial deviation is perhaps the best known, as the literature on "multi-level governance (MLG) (Hooghe, 1994; Marks *et al.*, 1996; Scharpf, 1997)." The temporal dimension of the deviations from linear, rational decision making as usually conceptualized can be captured by the idea of the "garbage can model" and the ideas of bounded rationality (Simon, 1947) that are inherent in that model. The organizational basis of deviation is a consequence of the network conceptualizations of policy making that we have been discussing. The logic here is that policy making is at least in part externalized from the state and hence faces problems of rectifying competing interests and maintaining legitimacy for actors not directly involved in the network.

Multilevel governance

While scholars and politicians familiar with federal political systems will find little that is novel in a political system that is characterized by multiple points of access and multiple decision makers, this aspect of the EU has created substantial intellectual interest. The fundamental point in this discussion is that policy making in the EU can no longer be seen as being centralized in Brussels, but rather now involves at least three levels of government—European, national, and regional/ local. The final choices about policy are made by the interaction of these levels of government, or the selection of which level will take the lead on a particular policy, is largely indeterminate and the object of negotiation. Rather than being structured by formal rules and constitutions, decision-making situations in MLG appear indeterminate and negotiable among the parties. The creation of a system such as the EU almost inevitably creates a multitiered decision arena such as this, but this property appears to have been increasing in the EU and now having the label of MLG makes it easier to discuss.

As well as providing empirical information concerning the nature of emerging patterns of governance in the EU, the literature on MLG has had a prominent normative element. This normative argument has been that the creation of the multilevel structures of decision making that has enhanced democracy by permitting alternative avenues for participation by groups and individuals. Interests that might be excluded in a more centralized regime are assumed to have an opportunity for access in the multilevel structures. That is perhaps especially true in a political structure such as the EU that is commonly argued to have a "democratic deficit" and in which democratic control over many central features of the policy-making process is at best weak. It is argued that by moving the locus of control over policy downward, and especially to the increasingly important regional level of government (Keating, 1998) more democratic control can be exercised.

The creation of the more open and indeterminate MLG arrangement within the EU may have some decided advantages for the system. This bargaining structure may be a way of ameliorating the effects of the "joint decision trap" than has been argued to plague the EU (Scharpf, 1988). If the rules of federal or other formats drive decisions toward the lowest common denominator, then optional points of access may provide a means of shifting the locus of debate and finding alternatives that can be more positive for all the actors involved. In addition, MLG may encourage the political participation of social and ethnic groups that have felt excluded from other aspects of the political process.

The creation of a more indeterminate process also may empower state organizations relative to social actors, simply because of their command of information and their (relatively) coherent policy preferences (see later). In a context of uncertainty any actor who can bring to the table some modicum of certainty and coherence, even if it is self-serving, has an advantage. Edgar Grande (1996) also has pointed to a "paradox of weakness" that exists within European policy making. His argument is that the apparent loss of power of state institutions in the European governance process is just that, and that the European political process has provided increased power to state actors to overcome the power of domestic constraints on their power.[11] Further, within the European apparatus itself MLG and the creation of less formally structured policy processes may privilege the Commission vis-à-vis other actors, because of the greater policy-making capacity within the Commission.[12]

Time, space, organization, and garbage cans

The "garbage can model" of decision making (Cohen *et al.*, 1972) which was discussed in Chapter 3 offers, we argue, a rewarding analytical tool in understanding MLG. As well as deviating from notions of linearity, determinacy, and the usual conceptions of rationality in the policy process along a spatial dimension, we can also conceptualize deviations occurring along a temporal dimension. That is, decisions cannot be made if all the requisite elements do not come together in time as well as space. The "garbage can model" demonstrates that decisions become possible when there is a confluence of the (largely independent) streams of problems, solutions, and opportunities. That confluence is not, however, certain and in many cases simply may not occur, or if it does occur it comes about as the result of the interventions of individual policy entrepreneurs (Kingdon, 1995). These entrepreneurs define and manage situations and are central to opening the "policy windows" during which time decisions become possible.

The decision situations at the heart of the concept of the garbage can model were described by Cohen, March, and Olsen as "organized anarchies"—not surprisingly universities were the principal exemplar. The description of life in an organized anarchy which is the trademark of the garbage can theory bears some resemblance to discussions of policy making in networked governments. In the conventional state-centric conception of governing, participation in the policy process is managed in one of several ways. Perhaps most important the principal players would be governmental actors, rather than actors from civil society, and they would be mandated to participate or would find it in their political or organizational interest to participate. To the extent that elements of civil society are involved in the policy process this tends to be state-led, rather than being the autonomous decisions by those actors themselves. That structuring of participation may be through pluralist selection of a limited number of quasi-official representatives of societal segments, or it may be more corporatist or corporate pluralist in which multiple interests are brought together. These corporatist structures are capable of creating more integrated preferences for the society. The segmentation that characterizes most governments can be alleviated.

Policy making in many industrial democracies, and perhaps also the EU, can be characterized rather well by the ideas of the garbage can model[13] with the decline of conventional participation in government, and especially the decline of organizational actors such as political parties. The decline of traditional forms of political participation, especially the declining relevance of political parties in many systems (Dalton and Wattenberg, 2000), have made inputs into the political process less predictable and more difficult to aggregate. Likewise, many decision processes within the government itself have been deinstitutionalized so that government has a more difficult time producing coherent and coordinated responses to challenges from the environment.

The garbage can tends to enhance the power of the already powerful actors and to reduce the influence of those groups that were already less influential. The absence of clear preferences within institutions as a whole, and the declining importance of institutional actors (including those usually responsible for inputs) may enhance the influence of actors who can articulate more or less coherent preferences, and who can bring a technology to which they are committed when they come to the bargaining table. Having some solution, even if it is not completely effective, is always a better bargaining position than having none. Indeed, MLG itself has many of the characteristics of the garbage can model, and the two major shifts in governance to some extent interact in European countries to reinforce the indeterminacy of policy making.

Networks and the structure of policy making

We now turn to the third element of the deviation from a linear, rationalist notion of policy making in government. We have already discussed the role of networks, albeit more from the perspective of their role in linking state and society. Here we turn more to the issue of the impact of networked relationships between state and society in governance. Given that we begin by characterizing these relationships as representing some deviation from the linear model of governing, there is some expectation that the argument is less than laudatory about that involvement in policy. There is a certain negative case to the argument, but again it is more in terms of the unintended consequences of the use of networks, rather than the laudable, and important, attempts to open policy making to a broader range of interests and to provide means for enhanced democratic control. As Colin Hay puts it rather nicely:

> Networking, or so it would appear, offers the potential to establish parameters of stability and predictability within an otherwise

unstable, disorderly, unpredictable, path-dependent and rapidly changing environment. (1998:33)

Networks and networking do have a benign image and are crucial elements in European governance, meaning here, both at the national and the Brussels levels. They represent a generic form of linkage between state and society, so that one could subsume the more restrictive forms of linkage such as corporatism. Within the literature that has grown up self-described as networks there is also the difference made between more loosely structured networks and more tightly defined policy communities (see Jordan and Schubert, 1992). For all of these modes of interaction between state and society there are a number of private and public sector organizations that interact around a policy issue or set of concerns.

In addition to the linkage function performed by networks, there is a clear policy-making role for these structures. Policy making through networks represents a substantial form of deviation from the linear and hierarchical form of government action that has been the basis of most thinking about governing. In particular, network logics when applied to policy making assume that the network is capable of making and implementing decisions to a great extent on its own, and that the state becomes something of a figure head that will politely validate the activities of the network.

When taken to the extreme, this view of the role of networking in policy leads to the "governance without government" conception described in Chapter 2. Even in the less extreme views (Kooiman, 1993) this conception of governance rather obviously tends to move the locus of decision away from government and toward society. This view of governance also makes a number of assumptions about the governing capacity of networks that may not be borne out in reality, especially when one attempts to preserve fundamental notions of accountability and representative democracy.[14] Indeed, some of the problems already mentioned concerning other changes in governance may appear in this setting as well.

One of the most important barriers to effective democratic governance faced by networks is the need to make decisions, and to resolve conflicting views about policy. Here networks are between a rock and a hard place. On the one hand, if the network tends toward the loosely defined and highly inclusive model of the "issue network" it will be open and democratic, but may encounter substantial difficulties in making decisions. As Schon and Rein (1994) have argued the participants in a policy debate may not have the same mental "frame" concerning a policy issue, and may therefore find it impossible even to agree upon the terms of reference for any discussion of that issue. The assumptions about networks having this capacity appear rather felicitous, but there appear to be relatively few structures for resolving conflicts, and especially conflicts over fundamental definitions of what the problem is, that may exist within networks.

On the other hand, if the decision (witting or not) is to opt for a more restrictive "policy community" or "epistemic community" (Zito, 2000) then the problems for networks are reversed. In these relatively exclusive structures there may be little disagreement about the nature of the problem or even about what constitutes "good policy" (on the inclusivity or exclusivity of networks see Schaap and Van Twist, 1997). Those difficulties will largely have been defined away from making membership in the community based, de facto if not de jure, on agreement with the explicit or implicit framework defining the community. Thus, these organizations may meet the decision-making criterion of governance but fail rather badly on the democratic criterion. Indeed, traditional public sector structures may perform substantially better on the democratic norm than will policy communities.

Daujberg and Marsh (1998) point to another problem with employing the logic of policy networks when taken in isolation from the state structures, and indeed the social structures, in which they are embedded. The problem is that these structures are largely indeterminate, even if one takes the more restrictive notion of the policy community. The policy process is always somewhat unpredictable but the increasing use of network structures tends to reduce further the predictability and institutionalization of the process. Therefore, to understand what occurs in the policy process requires either a well-developed theory of state behavior or one of individual level behavior, or perhaps both.

Given that shift in patterns of policy making that have been occurring in the EU and in national political systems, many of the same arguments employed above with reference to the garbage can model and MLG may be applied equally well with references to the use of networks. That is, loosening the formal institutional boundaries of the process may tend to intensify the dominance of some actors at the expense of others. Any process change is likely to affect the distribution of powers in a political system, but the ones we are discussing here tend to enhance the influence of just those social and political groups whose impact on policy network analysts and practical reformers may have sought to temper by opening the process to a wider range of involvement from within the social network.

Again, like some of the other changes from state-centric versions of governing, the emphasis on networks may tend to enhance the influences of public sector organizations, most obviously those within the bureaucracy. The central element of this argument is that networks, in order to be effective, must be connected to government organizations responsible for making policy. Networks without those connections are most unlikely to have any real influence over policy, and that in turn empowers the government organization in question to set the boundaries of membership and action. In some ways, the network models may de facto become a pluralist model with government organizations being able to sort out whom they want and do not want. Again, as Daujberg and Marsh point out, any attempt at understanding the functions of networks in the absence of an understanding of the state, is likely to be ineffective.

Conclusion

In this chapter, we have attempted to link the concepts of governance and governability with the changes in processes of policy making occurring in most of the advanced industrial democracies and also in the EU. The changes we have been identifying are manifested in the real world of policy making, and are also reflected within the academic theorizing that attempts to capture that reality. As a number of scholars have pointed out about European governance, many of the reforms implemented in the name of greater openness and democracy have often had unintended consequences, and may have reduced the actual level of involvement of social elements in the process of governing.

We have discussed the importance of institutions in society for the governability of the society, as well as the nature of institutional changes within the public sector that may or may not correspond with the society. The outcome of this analysis may appear excessively pessimistic. The purpose was not to be pessimistic, nor to be unjustifiably negative about some of the approaches to understanding policy making in contemporary governments. Rather, the purpose of the analysis is to stimulate thought about the implications of political change and to explore the interactions of an aspiration to open policy making to a wider range of influences with the political dynamics that changes in process appear to have engendered.

5
Multilevel Governance: A Faustian Bargain?

The restructuring of political authority in the Western European political and institutional context propelled by the growing powers of the EU has been fertile soil for analyses of MLG. The search for alternative accounts of intergovernmental relations has also been fuelled by regional devolution in countries such as some of the Scandinavian and Southern European states (notably Spain) and the UK (Pierre and Stoker, 2000). Relationships among institutions at different tiers of government in this perspective are believed to be fluid, negotiated, and contextually defined. Previously hierarchical models of institutional "layering," for example, formal treatments of federalism, are being replaced with a more complex image of intergovernmental relations in which subnational authorities engage in direct exchange with supranational or global institutions and vice versa.

There is little doubt that the continuing consolidation of the EU and the devolution of political power within the state entail changes in institutional relationships that challenge our traditional understanding of those relationships. That said, most of the analytical models and interpretations of MLG that we have seen so far have fallen in the same trap as some analyses of governance, that is, a previously state-centric and constitutional perspective has been almost completely replaced by an image of governing in which institutions are largely irrelevant (but see Bulmer, 1993; Jordan, 2001). We believe that this account of recent changes in intergovernmental relations is exaggerated at best, and misleading at worst. The institutional "grip" on political processes within the state and between domestic and supranational actors, although recently relaxed, remains strong and can be further strengthened by the state if and when considered necessary.

It is also frustrating to note the rather widespread notion that MLG is all about context, processes, and bargaining. The "shift" toward MLG should rather be conceived of as a gradual, incremental development in which institutions still play a defining role in governing. Institutions, not processes, are the vehicles of democratic and accountable government; hence we should only expect institutions not to surrender their leverage to contextually defined and ad hoc models of governing. While it is true that the challenge of governing has taken on a new magnitude along with the multi-"layering" of political institutions and authority, political control and accountability remain just as critical as ever to democratic government.

This chapter seeks to develop and sharpen existing theoretical models or conceptualizations of MLG. Although this concept is today frequently employed in a wide range of analytical contexts, we still lack both a clear conceptual analysis of such governance as well as a critical discussion MLG of as a democratic process. MLG is frequently misconceived or misunderstood, either with regard to process or to outcomes, or both. It has become a popular model of intergovernmental relationships, partly because it draws on informal and inclusive ideals of decision making and partly because it appears to be a cozy, consensual, and accommodative process. We are less sanguine. In particular, we argue that the absence of distinct legal frameworks and the reliance on sometimes quite informal negotiations between different institutional levels could well be a "Faustian bargain" where actors only see the attractions of the deal and choose to ignore the darker consequences of the arrangement. To some extent, the "Faustian bargain" stems from a tendency in MLG thinking that it represents something radically different from traditional models of intergovernmental relations. Thus, we argue that the "Faustian bargain" can be to some extent escaped if MLG is not seen as an alternative but rather as a complement to intergovernmental relations defined in a regulatory framework.

The growing scholarly interest in the emergence of new forms of governance during the past several years has more recently also been cast in an MLG analytical framework. Much of this analysis appeared first among EU scholars who sought to develop a framework for the analysis of the relationships between EU institutions, the state and subnational governments. While domestic multitier systems of governance were hierarchical in so far as communication, resources, steering, and control normally moved up or down through all levels in the hierarchy, in the EU context, transnational institutions frequently targeted subnational institutions thus sidestepping the level of the state.

In addition to adding another institutional tier to the traditional equation of intergovernmental relationships, there was also a strong notion that the nature of the relationships between these tiers was distinctly different from domestic relationships between the already existing tiers of institutions. Thus, MLG is assumed to differ from traditional intergovernmental relationships in three respects: it is focused on systems of governance involving transnational, national, and subnational institutions and actors; it highlights negotiations and networks, not constitutions and other legal frameworks, as the defining feature of institutional relationships; and it makes no *ex ante* judgments about a logical order between different institutional tiers.

We first conduct a conceptual analysis of MLG as there is a need to sort out in some detail MLG is and is not. Following that discussion, we critically assess it in terms of its alleged contribution and also— which has been largely absent in the debate so far—the perils and dangers associated with such governance in terms of participation, accountability, transparency, and inclusion. We have attempted to maintain a focus on questions such as these throughout this discussion of governance, and thinking about MLG should be no different. The third section presents a brief analysis of three cases as examples; the structural funds in the EU, intergovernmental relationships in the US, and recent institutional reform at the regional level in the UK.

Multilevel governance: what is it?

Our first task is to define exactly what is meant by MLG, at least for us in this discussion of the concept. There are four aspects of this concept that require some elaboration: the concept of governance itself as it appears in the MLG literature; the notion of governance that can include several levels of government; the negotiated order which characterizes the relationship among these multiple and often at least partially autonomous levels; and the notion of MLG as a particular form of political game.

The first and most obvious defining feature of MLG is that it is governance; we share Smith's frustration of the fact that most approaches to MLG have a "paradoxical focus on government rather than governance" (Smith, 1997:725). That is to say, this concept should refer to a broader, more inclusive, and encompassing process of coordination than the conventional view of government. The common denominator in definitions of governance is that the term refers to the process through which public and private actions and resources are coordinated and given a common direction and meaning.

The significance of these defining features of governance in the present context is that unlike traditional models of intergovernmental relationships, MLG refers to connected processes of governance incorporating both public and private actors in contextually defined forms of exchange and collaboration. The institutional dimension of MLG remains critical, partly because it is institutions that define the linkages between different levels of government, partly because institutions as actors on one or more than one level help coordinate MLG, and partly because MLG—as all types of governance—is embedded in institutional webs which "shape and constrain" political action (March and Olsen, 1989).

Second, the concept of MLG refers to a particular kind of relationship between several institutional levels. The basic idea here is that in MLG, actors, arenas, and institutions are not ordered hierarchically but have a more complex and contextually defined relationship. As Marks and his associates put it,

> political arenas are interconnected rather than nested . . .
> Subnational actors . . . operate in both national and supranational arenas, creating transnational associations in the process. States do not monopolize links between domestic and European actors, but are one among a variety of actors contesting decisions that are made at a variety of levels . . . The separation between domestic and international politics, which lies at the heart of the state-centric model [of EU governance], is rejected by the MLG model. (Marks *et al.*, 1996:346–7)

Thus, MLG theory argues that although local authorities are embedded in regional and national webs of rules, resources, and patterns of coordination, these webs do not prevent them from pursuing their interests at global arenas. The notion of "embeddedness" should not be seen as the complete opposite to the hierarchical model of intergovernmental relationships but it does signify that lower-level institutions are not invariably constrained by higher-level institutions' decisions and actions. Hierarchy has to a significant extent been replaced by a division of labor, competence, and jurisdiction among largely self-regulatory governance processes at different tiers of government.

Similarly, competencies and jurisdictions are increasingly defined at one institutional level only and not—as was previously often the case—as sectoral "silos" where central, regional, and local government had clearly defined roles and relationships to each other. Indeed, it could be argued that hierarchy has been replaced by stratarchy, an organizational model where each level of the organization operates to a large extent independently of other organizational levels. For example, as a result of the decentralization in Western Europe, local and regional authorities today are less monitored by central government compared to a decade or so ago. Instead, central government agencies tend to concentrate on exchanges within central government while local and regional authorities receive "lump grants" from the state to be spent largely on their discretion. There is some similarity to this pattern in the US where the "New Federalism" launched in the 1980s served to give the states some of their historical autonomy in relationship to the federal government. In both cases, it makes more sense to talk about a division of labor among institutions at different levels than a hierarchy.

Governance including several institutional levels raises the question of what constitutes the linkages between these levels. While individual actors can occasionally serve as such linkages, the most important continuous linkage between different levels of governance is institutions. These institutions can play either a direct or an indirect linking role; they can either themselves, as political authorities, operate at multiple levels; or, they can, in the shape of arenas for political actors, indirectly facilitate this type of linkage. Either way, however, is seems clear that it is only institutions that can provide continuous linkages between governance at different levels of the system. This institutional linkage often evolves in the shape of what Painter (2001) refers to as "concurrent competencies," that is, situations where the jurisdiction of institutions at different levels overlap to a smaller or larger extent.

Needless to say, the institutional arrangements and relationships that are said to be typical of MLG differ from traditional intergovernmental relationships in several important respects. True, central government in most Western countries have relaxed some of their previous political and/or financial control over subnational authorities, but this decentralization has not been critical to the emergencè of MLG. Since most of these states have also sought to "hive off" financial responsibilities to local governments (Sharpe, 1988) it has become clear to subnational authorities that future strategies of resource mobilization should not be targeted at the state but should look elsewhere for financial resources (Le Galés and Harding, 1998). This is part of the explanation as to why international initiatives have become a popular strategy among local and regional authorities in several countries (e.g., Beauregard and Pierre, 2000; Fry, 1998; Hobbs, 1994).

Moreover, MLG could be said to be a way of capitalizing on the growing professionalism of regional and local authorities. Their increasing assertiveness vis-à-vis central government in many jurisdictions is proof of a self-reliance that stems in part from having the administrative and organizational capabilities to make autonomous decisions regarding their resource mobilization strategies without having to submit to the central state. Indeed, in many countries—Germany and Belgium for example—subnational governments have modernized more rapidly and effectively than have central governments and are more capable of managing policies than is the central government. This reversal of the usual balance of capabilities alters the conduct of politics and presses toward the type of networked and largely inchoate pattern associated with MLG.

All of this having been said, however, it should also be noted that the constitutional definitions of institutional competencies have remained remarkably intact; apart from the decentralization mentioned earlier, we have seen very few cases of constitutional reform accompanying the emergence of MLG. Subnational authorities launching ambitious international initiatives, even up to the point of signing agreements with overseas authorities, do so in violation with the constitutional definition of their competencies (Beauregard and Pierre, 2000). It is difficult to see how long any major discrepancy between the formal and de facto definitions of institutional discretion can be sustained.

A third feature of MLG is that it denotes a negotiated order rather than an order defined by formalized legal frameworks (Kohler-Koch, 1996; Scharpf, 1997). To some extent, the negotiated nature of MLG is a reflection of the "nested" nature of the institutional arrangements; the breakup of traditional hierarchies has disrupted the previous more distinct patterns of command and control (Pierre and Stoker, 2000:31). More importantly, however, multilevel exchanges in cases where supranational institutions such as the EU are still in the process of developing their jurisdiction and their agenda tend to relate to actors and institutions in their external environment through negotiations. Stated slightly differently, institutionalization entails negotiation; the evolving nature of the EU necessitates a reliance on negotiations rather than resorting to some formal, constitutional power bases which are yet to be given their final design.

Therefore, to some extent MLG represents a transnational version of the familiar network ideas employed to understand the domestic level of governance. The similarity can be seen in several features. One is that there are multiple linkages of actors, with little or no hierarchical structure among the actors. In addition, these are negotiated arrangements in which there is little or no capability to predict outcomes in advance. Further, as in some treatments of networks, these structures may be self-referential and resist attempts to impose order, whether from without or from within.

Finally, MLG is frequently conceived of as a political game. This notion refers less to a rational-choice inspired approach to MLG but more to the idea that the relaxation of regulatory frameworks opens up more strategic and autonomous behavior among the actors. Another important aspect of the game-like nature of governance, as opposed to the conventional view of intergovernmental relationships, is that the definition of who is a player becomes an empirical question as does the definition of the stakes. Further, as in networks of all sorts playing the game may be as important as winning in each iteration of the game. Therefore, MLG can be associated with some moderation of demands by actors in order to maintain their favored position as players.

Any game must have actors, and one of the characteristics of MLG is that it is a game that many players can play simultaneously. The game extends well beyond Putnam's (1983) concept of a two-level game in which bargainers on the international level are to some extent constrained by domestic politics. In the MLG game institutions from several levels of government may be engaged in bargaining over policy, each institution bringing with it a set of goals that may or may not be congruent with those of the other players. Further, the goals may be institutional as well as substantive. That is, subnational governments may be using this governance process, and the arenas created by it, as a means of evading control from central government, and EU institutions may also conceive of this process as a means of enhancing their own powers vis-à-vis national governments.

This is primarily a governmental and institutional game, so that the major players and the major goals are those of the political entities involved rather than private sector actors that may have a concern about the substantive policies. This means that it is more difficult to restrict access to the game than if there were only interest groups or individuals who wanted to participate. Once in, however, the alignments of the players may not be readily predictable so that there is a real game. That is, on some issues the alignments may be by institutional level within the political system while on others players may align according to partisan control of the government, or perhaps functional or regional interests. Where the EU is concerned, it has some advantages as a player given that it has fewer political constraints and therefore may be freer to play without concern for the two- or three-level game concerns of national or subnational governments.

What multilevel governance is not

We now have developed a general idea about what MLG is and the range of phenomena to which it refers. In order to take the definitional discussion further—and to sort out some of the apparent confusion over various manifestations of MLG—we now focus more closely on intergovernmental patterns more broadly. This enables us to see where the MLG model clearly differs from competing conceptualizations of such institutional relations.

First, it is clear, as has already been suggested, that MLG does not refer to intergovernmental relations as usually conceived. MLG has a wider cast of actors than traditional models of intergovernmental relations; here, we should expect to see public as well as nonpublic actors to be involved in governance. "Nonpublic" actors is shorthand for a wide variety of actors that have an interest in participating in any given governance process, such as private businesses, voluntary associations, organized interests, or single-issue pressure groups. Since one of the defining features of governance is the pooling of public and private resources toward collective goals and interests, we should expect a significant diversity of actors to be involved in governance. This diversity of actors adds an intriguing complexity to MLG, as some nonpublic actors tend to be almost as hierarchically structured and vertically integrated as systems of political institutions. For instance, organized interests in the environmental policy sector are frequently involved in governance at the local, regional, national, and supranational levels. Thus the diversity of actors tends to create multiple linkages between governance processes at different levels.

Second, MLG should not be conceived of as a hierarchical order of governance processes. Instead, MLG sees transnational institutions engaging in direct communication with subnational actors, or vice versa. MLG is thus not controlled from above as tends to be the rule in hierarchical systems. This absence of authority, coupled with the search for the definition of competencies—or the management of overlapping competencies—creates institutional exchanges which are typically ad hoc and designed differently for each specific matter.

Not very surprisingly, actors at different institutional levels have very different interpretations of this type of governance. At the local level, the idea of being able to negotiate directly with powerful and resourceful transnational institutions is extremely appealing. For instance, regions within the EU, which have experienced increasing difficulties in mobilizing financial resources from the state, attach great hopes to their exchange with the EU structural funds. Similarly, transnational institutions enjoy the possibility to choose whether to approach national or subnational institutions, according to the nature of the specific problem at hand. Instead, it is actors at the national level which tend to be the main critics of this arrangement; they lose some of their previous control over subnational institutions at the same time as they have to conform policies, rules, and programs to international institutions. Thus, the view of the consequences of MLG from the central government level is rather bleak. While central governments may see power draining away as a result of this process it may also have positive aspects. In particular, the bargaining may make more explicit the transnational political processes that are in train. Therefore, some more explicit recognition of MLG may benefit a government that stands to lose hierarchical control. Further, given that the coalitions in these bargaining relationships are fluid and subject to a number of influences, national governments may be able to create coalitions to oppose either Brussels or their own subnational governments, depending upon the issues at hand and the bargaining capabilities of national elites. Playing a more bilateral game may make the task of a central government seeking to maintain its position, or some portion thereof, more difficult.

Furthermore, MLG could be seen as proof of the increasing mutual dependency that characterizes institutional exchanges in the contemporary state (Rhodes, 1997). Several decades ago, central governments could exercise close political and economic control of subnational authorities within their nominal domain. Lately, some of that control has been relaxed; institutions have entered a relationship which recognizes that central government, while still the unrivalled locus of political power, has much to gain from acquiring advice from institutions at lower tiers of government.

All of this having been said, it is also important to note that MLG theory sometimes tends to exaggerate the hierarchical and legal nature of intergovernmental relationships prior to the emergence of this model of governing. There are several accounts of intergovernmental relationships in different national contexts which highlight the negotiated nature of the relationship between the state and local government (Ashford, 1990; Gustafsson, 1987; Rhodes, 1986). Some degree of negotiation and informal advice has always characterized institutional exchanges and it is fair to assume that this institutional exchange has played a critical role in enhancing the efficiency and coordination of the institutional system. Even so, however, MLG differs from such contextually defined institutional relationships in two important respects; new (horizontal) models of governance have emerged at each of these institutional levels and, moreover, the previously rather strict hierarchical ordering of institutions has been down played.

Third, MLG is sometimes believed to be "post-constitutional" or "extra-constitutional." The processes that have emerged (often without formal planning or formal sanction) are not constrained by formal agreements or rules, although inevitably they can run up against formal barriers and limits on jurisdictions. Thus, these processes are more than federalism and more like the processes of "intergovernmental politics" described by Deil Wright (1989; see also Walker, 1999) and other students of the changing nature of American "federalism." The arguments made by these scholars are that the informal bargaining has become at least as important as the formal allocations of power among levels, and that politics rather than laws and formal structural arrangements is the determining factor for outcomes. This once again describes a political process that is less determinate than a system of hierarchical subordination, but also a system that may have the flexibility to adapt to changing requirements.

Finally, a defining feature of MLG is that it is a model of governing which largely defies, or ignores, structure. As in most other accounts of governance, the focus is clearly on process and outcomes. The process of governing does not have a uniform pattern but is defined differently owing to the nature of the policy problem and the institutional location of key actors. Indeed, the informality and absence of structural constraints that characterizes MLG is often seen as some of its most attractive features since this is believed to produce a more accommodative and efficient governance. Thus, in MLG, structures are not determinate of outcomes as can be the case in domestic politics (Weaver and Rockman, 1993); the empirical institutional explanation has little to offer to an understanding of MLG.

Summary: political complexity and indeterminate policy outcomes

The joint outcome of globalization, decentralization, deregulation, and agentification has been erosion of traditional bases of political authority. Furthermore, although democratic government still resorts to its traditional institutional setup, contemporary governance seems to bypass or ignore traditional definitions of authority: the realities of governance seem to escape the boundaries of the nation-state. Modern nation-states are neither all-powerful nor autonomous externally; the domains of administration, politics, and international relations are intertwined in ways that considerably complicate their description and effective governance within them (March and Olsen, 1995:123). MLG theory shares March and Olsen's views on the discrepancy between governance and the constitutional map of political life.

The analysis so far raises two questions. The first question relates to the challenge which emerging forms of governance, not least MLG, pose to the traditional institutions of the state. What is at stake here is our understanding of governance (see Peters, 2000a); we can either conceive of emerging patterns as "new governance" and ask questions about whether coordination is attained, or, in the "old governance" perspective, ask questions about how the traditional institutional system of the state is geared to participate in governance. MLG, like all forms of governance, clearly offers some degree of political congruence in a complex web of institutions, actors, and interests. But is MLG the outcome of political deliberation, and how do we hold it to political account? Has problem-solving capacity (Scharpf, 1997) and outcomes taken precedence over democratic input and accountability?

The other related question addresses the consequences of governance that "escapes" traditional boundaries and regulatory frameworks. The present authors question the cozy, accommodative nature of MLG as it emerges in much of the literature. In particular, we believe that MLG, while tempting and attractive in its informality and orientation toward objectives and outcomes rather than focused on rules and formal arrangements, could be a "Faustian bargain" in which core values of democratic government are traded for accommodation, consensus, and the purported increased efficiency in governance. Many regulatory frameworks were implemented in order to define the rights and entitlements of constituencies vis-à-vis the state and each other. Additionally, much of the regulation and legislation that states have enacted has been aimed at changing social behavior; environmental policies and gender equality policies are two cases in point. An assessment of the benefits of relaxing existing rules must depart from recognition of the political nature of regulation (Horwitz, 1986). Thus, informal patterns of political coordination could in fact be a strategy for political interests to escape or bypass regulations put in place explicitly to prevent that from happening.

Multilevel governance: the Faustian bargain?

On its face the content of MLG appears very benign, and as a recognition of many continuing processes of democratization in the European countries and within the EU. Unlike some approaches to policy making in Europe (and in individual nation-states), MLG is inclusive and tends to assume that including more actors does not diminish the capacity to reach decisions. Therefore, for democratic reasons the system can be opened to a range of actors.

Also, the assumption of many of the scholars working in this approach is that decision making will be nonconflictual and accommodative. Again, this is a benign assumption but may not capture the reality of the processes involved. After all, bargaining must be about something and it is likely that there will be divergent interests among the participants. In some societies one might expect these differences to be worked out in a relatively consensual manner, but that political style does not appear to hold for European politics. Most of the evidence is that actors in Brussels are working very hard to defend their interests (national or sectoral) in very tough bargaining arenas (Kassim *et al.*, 2000). Therefore, it appears excessively optimistic to assume that the bargaining can be accomplished without real conflict of interests, and therefore the use of means other than sweet reason to reach decisions.

Following from the above, the assumption in the discussion of MLG has been that the outcomes of the processes are bargained and not imposed. Again, that is a benign assumption and perhaps largely true. Although true at one level, the bargaining processes may well hide a good deal of power. First, there is the power to set the agenda for the discussions, something that remains largely in the hands of central governments. Further, within the context of the EU the choice of institutional locale for the crucial aspects of debate may shift powers in one direction or another—but usually away from the subnational governments. Whether at the council level that advantages national governments or the commission level that advantages the EU itself, the regional and/or local governments are likely to find their interests less well represented.

Even if the assumptions about MLG were completely correct, there might well still be difficulties in the bargain that has been struck. These problems concern more the governance aspects of the equation than the multilevel aspects. That is, can this arrangement really provide governance, meaning as we indicated earlier the steering of a society or a set of societies toward some common goals? In the first instance, it appears that goal setting through means other than imposition is difficult. This is, in fact, always the case and determining goals is often a centralizing aspect of any political process.

In addition, having removed or simply not adopted formal means of making decisions, there are few means of resolving conflicts among the participants. The rather happy assumption, similar to that contained in most network theory, is that there is some commonality of purposes and means of achieving those purposes among the participants in an MLG process. That may happen, but it is not necessarily the most likely event. Indeed, there might be little need for these processes if there were so much agreement among the actors about means and ends. Therefore, the outcomes of MLG processes are likely to be either conflicts that have to be resolved in other venues, or "pork-barrel" agreements that give everybody something and do not necessarily resolve the fundamental policy problems that produced the need for the bargaining in the first place.

Another, and arguably more serious problem associated with MLG is that the alleged cozy and consensual nature of this arrangement in fact is a consensus dictated by the stronger players. Formal and legal arrangements are often seen as excessively complicating and rigid frameworks for political decision making, but one of their virtues is that they do delineate power relationships and often provide the less powerful with formal means of combating the more powerful. With those constraints removed, or at least de-emphasized the more powerful players—usually national governments—may be able to dominate the processes. These national governments may themselves have difficulties in agreeing on goals and desired outcomes, and these differences may create opportunities for subnational governments to achieve some of their goals, but the process remains one that will be dominated by the more powerful. It could well be that the outcome of MLG is a benign model of governing for all concerned; the point is that we have no guarantees that it will be benign. Just as constitutions in many countries, notably the US, rest on a distrust of the benevolence of resourceful political actors, so does the absence of any clear and comprehensive rules for institutional exchange in MLG raise questions about its ability to cater to the interests of weak actors.

Another way of understanding this problem is to consider to what extent informality entails inequality. Formal rules serve, inter alia, an important role in safeguarding equality in terms of the capabilities of the actors. For example, constitutional principles tend to ensure the same equality of power for all states or provinces in a federal structure. True, such equality can be safeguarded by less coercive instruments, but informality basically means that it is incumbent upon the actors themselves to permit different actors to participate and to de facto define their relative leverage. For instance, (informal) MLG in the context of the EU may generate significant differences among different local and regional authorities with regard to their access to EU funds owing to differences in their political access or their ability to launch campaigns to lobby within the EU.

We should also ask to what extent informality entails outcomes reflecting the status quo and/or the interests of dominant players. It could be argued that the legitimacy of MLG is contingent on broad political and institutional support which, in turn, depends on the extent to which MLG caters to the interests of all actors. In the EU, therefore, MLG may in practice favor the interests of the nation-states as the dominant players, even though it is conceptualized as providing greater power to the structurally less powerful subnational actors. Again, however, we find that informality will respond to the interests of weaker constituencies if and when dominant players find a reason to do so.

Although MLG has some severe problems for governments in the real world, political analysts are perhaps in even greater peril of losing their souls by accepting this doctrine. While MLG has the virtue of being capable of being invoked in almost any situation, that is also its great problem. Any complex and multifaced political process can be referred to as MLG. Second, and perhaps more importantly, MLG appears incapable of providing clear predictions or even explanations (other than the most general) of outcomes in the governance process. As already noted, this approach has some similarities with network analysis, and one of those similarities is its indeterminate nature. It is very nice to say that a range of actors were involved and negotiated a solution but we would argue that a more definitive set of predictions are needed.

Why is this a Faustian bargain? The argument is that the capacity to govern has been sold, or at least has been downgraded, in an attempt to achieve more open and inclusive bargaining, and in order to circumvent formal structures that have been central to governing and to intergovernmental allocations in many systems. On the one hand that may not be possible, especially when the players involved may be relatively new and rather jealous of their prerogatives. On the other hand, if it is possible then the system of governing that is implied may not really be a system of governing.

Examples of the bargain: two cases

We have now presented an argument that the bargains being struck in the context of MLG are "Faustian." This argumentation has been largely by assertion, and we should present at least some more empirical evidence to justify those assertions. The following are two cases, drawn from rather different levels of development of the bargains, that illustrate the difficulties of making MLG perform as intended, even for federal societies that are accustomed to intergovernmental bargaining and complex governance structures.

Multilevel governance and the case of the European Union structural funds

The structural funds in the EU have been used as examples of MLG within the EU. These funds represent a major political and economic commitment of the Union, surpassed only by agricultural support. The funds target different types of structural problems, such as infrastructural development in rural or coastal regions or support for enhanced telecommunications (Smith, 1997). Given the regional or local nature of the targets for the funds, the EU invites applications from regions or cities and allocates resources directly to regions and locales. Member-states and their governments thus have very little to do with the allocation of these funds. In many ways, this process epitomizes MLG; it includes several different institutional levels, exchanges between these levels are characterized more by negotiations than by hierarchical exchanges, and EU institutions bypass the member-state government level.

This type of policy design is appropriate and logical, given that the problems which the funds are employed to resolve vary from one region to another, even within the same country. Thus there is basically no function or need for the member-state governments to be involved in the allocation or implementation of the funds. Furthermore, concentrating on subnational authorities is consistent with the philosophy of a "Europe of the Regions." While the recent constitutional debate within the EU seems to downplay the significance of regions it remains the case that in terms of the structural funds we should expect regions to be the main policy target also in the foreseeable future.

However, this policy design has several important consequences with respect to its impact on intergovernmental relationships within the member-states. One is that it tends to empower regions vis-à-vis central government (Smyrl, 1997). This is primarily because regions becomes less dependent on regional economic support from central authorities and also because the EU has proven to be an important arena for regional authorities to mobilize resources not just from the structural funds but also from other institutions such as the Committee of the Regions. Furthermore, the policy design of the EU structural funds requires regional and local authorities to forge coalitions or partnerships with private businesses and their organizations. The structural funds are specifically used to enhance governance at the regional or local levels. If successful, this development tends to strengthen the region vis-à-vis central government by virtue of more concerted and effective economic development strategies.

Do the structural funds represent a good illustration of the "Faustian bargain"? Well, yes and no. Yes, insofar as the funds represent a significant financial inflow into regions and locales which the central government has effectively speaking no control over. In some countries—Britain being one example—regional support from the EU has led the central government to reduce its regional support with the same amount according to the so-called additionality principle which needless to say has been the source of major disagreement between regional authorities and central political institutions. There is an element of a "Faustian bargain" here to the extent that the MLG-style of allocating structural funds raises questions about coordination and accountability.

Overall, however, the case of the structural funds seems to entail only few of the problems discussed earlier regarding problems of democracy, equal strength among participants, and so on. There are several reasons for this. One is that this case of MLG is not concerned with political decision making or even representation. Instead, it is more a matter of how best to allocate resources to improve and upgrade the infrastructure, broadly defined, in the member-states. Second, given the requirement that fund recipients must present a public–private partnership which will implement the funds at the regional or local level, the impact of the funds in terms of democracy and governance appears to, if anything, be primarily to strengthen inclusion transparency and not to jeopardize such values. Thus, as this and the other case studies in this chapter suggest, the "Faustian bargain" nature of MLG seems to be related primarily to cases of institutional exchange where political representation and decision making are at stake and less so when the multilevel exchange is concerned with the implementation of EU policies and programs.

Multilevel governance and the North American Free Trade Area

Most of the discussion of MLG has been conducted with respect to the EU, perhaps because of the novelty (at least in unitary governments) of having multiple power centers in European politics.[1] The same issues have arisen, albeit in the guise of intergovernmental relations (Simeon and Cameron, 2000; Wright, 1989), in the federal systems of the US, Canada, and Mexico. Although there is a long history of complex formats for governance in these federal countries, the level of complexity has been increased by the creation of the North American Free Trade Area (NAFTA) that involves the three large North American systems.

NAFTA is by no means as pervasive an example of MLG as is the EU, but it does create, and enhance, that style of governing within North America. It does add another level of organization creating rules with a binding effect on citizens, and even other governments. At the same time, the subnational governments as well as national governments are accustomed to exerting a good deal of influence over policy. All those levels of government are accustomed also to complex political interactions among themselves as they negotiate for that influence as well as for financial resources. In short, they were in the business of MLG long before the term had been invented.

The MLG being created in North America represents some interesting contrasts to that being created through the EU. In the first place, the relationship among the nations involved is more asymmetric than in the EU, with the US having a much more disproportionate share of the economic clout within NAFTA (Payne, 2000). Indeed, the creation of a formalized arrangement such as NAFTA may be crucial for reducing that power and creating more of a level playing field for all three countries. The negotiations that produced the agreement were largely asymmetric, but yet the need to reach a bargain did generate greater equality than might otherwise be possible.

Another important characteristic of NAFTA as an example of MLG is that all the levels of government involved are familiar with having some latitude for autonomous action. This is perhaps less true for the states in Mexico than for subnational governments in the other two countries, but even in that case the formal nature of the federalism does provide some power.[2] Canada, on the other hand, is one of the most decentralized federations in the world so that the provinces are used to having substantial influence. Further, in both countries local governments have developed their own lines of involvement with national governments, bypassing the intermediate level, and inter-acting directly with the national government and constituting one of the most powerful interest groups in those countries. Finally, the governments involved in the NAFTA arrangements are themselves far from unitary actors. This is true to some extent for all governments but is perhaps especially true for the US It has a strong and deeply ingrained pattern of policy making through decentralized agency and departmental structures, so that the Department of State and the Drug Enforcement Agency may be running rather different foreign policies at the same time. Thus, although regional structures such as the EU and NAFTA tend to be centralizing and to require mechanisms for coordination (Kassim *et al.*, 2000), NAFTA has not yet come close to producing that type of change in American government. This, in turn, means that more than in other MLG arrangements there is a major problem of coordination across policy areas as well as among the member-states (see also Peters, 1999).

The above discussion of bargaining and policy making within NAFTA presents a rather benign view of processes. In systems that have been accustomed to employing decentralized means of governing the new Continental level of policy making may be accommodated without excessive difficulty. On the other hand, policy making in environmental politics has been argued by some analysts, and many critics, to be a clear example of the Faustian nature of MLG that we have been discussing (Bennett, 1995; Hufbauer *et al.*, 2000). That is, the movement of some locus of control away from national govern-ments to the international body is argued to have weakened the degree of democratic control over this important policy area, and especially on the US–Mexico border to have resulted in substantial degradation.

Does the case of NAFTA correspond to our concept of the Faustian bargain in MLG? In some ways the North American version of intergovernmental connections is less "Faustian" given the long history of intergovernmental relations in these systems. Further, the relationships among the actors are to some extent more structured than in most other arrangements, given the presence of a dominant actor in the "network" that exists among these systems. In other ways, however, this agreement presents many of the problems identified in other cases of MLG, especially in the loss of accountability and control to rather amorphous institutions and agreements. To use yet another allusion, in this case at least MLG may be Janus faced as much as it is Faustian.

Conclusions: how do we save our souls?

The account of MLG presented here may appear excessively bleak and pessimistic. We believe, however, that MLG, both as a real-world phenomenon and as a scholarly model, needs to be critically assessed in order to facilitate a debate regarding its outcomes. Clearly, there is much in MLG suggesting that it has a high problem-solving capacity and that it is likely to generate efficient outcomes. That said, it also has features, which call its democratic nature into question. This refers primarily to the fuzzy instruments of accountability and political control. If MLG is a Faustian bargain, how do we save our souls, that is, how do we achieve the positive sides of the bargain without experiencing the downsides of the agreement? Unfortunately, the debate on MLG—as the debate on governance more generally— has to some degree been framed in dichotomies; the novelty that has been said to be typical of governance exaggerates the extent to which it differs from the conventional system of government. On closer inspection, it becomes clear that for the most part intergovernmental relations in most advanced states have always been characterized by two concurrent types of exchanges; a formal, constitutionally defined exchange and an informal, contextually defined exchange. Most intergovernmental relations probably require both of these exchanges to operate efficiently. Informal exchange helps explain the more formal communications and help lower-tier institutions implement decisions by institutions higher up in the hierarchy. By the same token, high-level institutions need information about how their policies work "on the ground" in order to design future policies. Thus, alongside the formal exchange there is a mutual need between institutions at different tiers of government for some kind of informal exchange. More importantly, however, all actors have the option to resort to the constitutional definition of their institutional capability if and when believed to be necessary to safeguard important institutional interests. Thus, what makes the informal exchanges efficient is that it is embedded in a regulatory framework.

Scholars of intergovernmental relations have long acknowledged the importance of the types of informal exchanges among levels of government that we have been identifying here (see, for instance, Wright, 1989). The debate on MLG probably has much to learn from the large existing literature on intergovernmental relations, as broadly defined, in the US and other countries. MLG embedded in a regulatory setting which enables weaker actors to define a legal basis for their action might be the best strategy to escape the Faustian bargain and to cheat darker powers.

6
Subordination or Partnership?: Changing Institutional Relationships in Comparative Perspective

Recent changes in intergovernmental relationships in the Western democracies offer plenty of useful illustrations to the discussion on the role of political institutions in increasingly complex political and economic settings. To be sure, from the point of view of central government it could even be argued that these recent changes exacerbate the messiness of governance rather than helping to manage complexity. The wave of decentralization that has swept across the Western world is to some extent proof of a growing need among political institutions to increase their points of contact and exchange with the surrounding society. However, in implementing these reforms central government has also put itself in the awkward position of significantly reducing its abilities to control subnational government. This chapter looks more closely at how these developments in intergovernmental relationships relate to the management of complexity and the extent to which these emerging institutional arrangements could be seen as part of the problem or of the solution.

Intergovernmental relationships have been subject to a rapidly growing interest among practitioners as well as academics. Most scholars agree that the previously predominant hierarchies structuring intergovernmental relations are softening and losing much of their former strength. In their place, more complex systems of negotiated and contextually defined institutional relationships are evolving. Those scholars, and many practitioners, also assume that previous models of hierarchical governance are gradually being replaced by less formal and more inclusive arrangements such as networks and partnerships (Pierre and Peters, 2000; Rhodes, 1997) that also involve actors in the private sector. Similarly, the relationships between political institutions at different levels has been described more as one of a division of labor with overlapping or concurrent competencies (Painter, 2001) and less as one where higher levels command and control lower levels.

Placed alongside other significant developments such as the predominant regime of economic deregulation in most Western democracies and the associated phenomenon of economic globalization, these new forms of intergovernmental relationships have contributed to fuelling the debate on the future of the nation-state. The state, it has been argued in this context, is thus challenged both from above and below and significant parts of its power have thus been displaced to other institutional levels.

The demise of the state is hardly a novel argument (Navari, 1991). Indeed, as we and others have pointed out (Evans, 1997; Mann, 1997; Pierre, 2000; Pierre and Peters, 2000; Weiss, 1998), the intriguing question is not so much to what extent the state is declining but rather how recent changes in intergovernmental relationships (including the consolidation of transnational organizations like the EU) have affected the state's ability to implement its programs and how the role of institutions at different levels in that process have changed during the past 10–15 years. Further, the powers of the transnational organizations are being extended to include bargaining relationships with subnational organizations that further alter any hierarchies that may have existed across levels of government.

The main argument in this chapter is that the increasing emphasis on governance—as shorthand for processes intended to bring together political institutions, private businesses, voluntary associations, and other important actors in society—at different institutional levels has weakened the hierarchical structure of most Western political systems. While much attention has been paid to the emergence of MLG, especially within the EU (see Chapter 5), we should also be aware that the development of governance at the regional and local levels strengthens political institutions at these levels vis-à-vis the central government.

Intergovernmental relations as multilevel governance

The development toward MLG could be seen as the final step in a longer process of changes in policy style and institutional behavior in contemporary democracies. Earlier in this book we have discussed governance either at the level of the nation-state or as a multilevel process of vertical and horizontal policy coordination. Governance, however, is a policy style emphasizing inclusion, partnership, a broad (i.e., public and private) mobilization of resources and—to put it even more broadly—concerted efforts in the pursuit of collective goals emerged primarily at the local level. To some extent this emergence of local governance was explained by the vast institutional fragmentation, or what Leach and Percy-Smith (2001:13) call " 'the sheer messiness' of local government" in Britain. Also, reducing conflict between political authorities and the local business community and to create incentives for cooperative and joint projects was a key element of the Thatcherite project in the 1980s and early 1990s (Anderson, 1990; Harding, 1998; Leach and Percy-Smith, 2000). It was not only the UK, however, in which the governance style became important at the local level before becoming evident at the level of the state.

Governance is also an increasingly important feature of the regional level of government. The regional level of the polity was for a long period of time a "forgotten" level of the unitary state (see Wright, 1998). Powerful regions have, historically speaking, been a feature of federal states. However, two developments have placed regions in unitary states at the forefront of institutional reform. In economic development, problems were conceived of either as local issues—that is, related to individual companies—or matters of national concern, primarily the management of declining industrial sectors. Over time, it has become increasingly obvious that the spatial distribution of industrial sectors is a key factor in economic development (see, for instance, Evans and Harding, 1997; Markusen, 1987); structural change in an industrial sector has different ramifications on different regions depending on the location of the industry. Since much of the mature manufacturing industry tends to be concentrated with a very limited number of regions in a given country, the confluence of economic sector and political region has highlighted the need to address matters of industrial structural change at the regional rather than at the local level. Furthermore, individual locales are also increasingly often seen as embedded in the regional economy. The current interest in industrial clusters and inserting the local economy into such clusters as an objective of local economic development is proof of the growing significance of regions.

Perhaps more importantly, however, regions became the key recipients for financial resources from the structural funds of the EU. Also, the constitutional philosophy of the EU designed to build a "Europe of the Regions" (see Le Galès and Lequesne, 1998) has propelled institutional reform at the regional institutional level. Since the structural funds explicitly promote cooperative strategies between the public sector and the business community, regional governance has become a key political and institutional objective for the European member-states. There is much to suggest that the structural funds have strengthened the regions, internally as well as with regard to the political relationship between the state and the region (Smyrl, 1997).

At the level of the nation-state, finally, several West European democracies emphasized an "enabling" policy style during the 1990s. The "enabling" state, in brief, is a state which defines its role in society as one of removing obstacles to economic growth. More broadly, the "enabling state" is less intervening, less steering, and less proactive than a state pursuing a more traditional policy style. No longer was government itself to be a direct economic actor, but rather was to support the development of private industry in its regions. Thus, the policy style of the "enabling state" was part and parcel of the predominant public policy in Western Europe during the past decade or so, based in opening up for markets, deregulation, and reducing the scope of the public sector. Also, the notion of the "enabling state" fits nicely with a governance perspective on the role of the state in society, emphasizing collaborative projects with the state as the chief structure in the pursuit of collective goals.

As we argued in Chapter 5, MLG in Western Europe has a distinct transnational component. It is impossible to discuss MLG without mentioning the EU and especially its links with regionalization. The EU is a key player in European MLG, partly because it is one of the levels involved in such governance and partly because it promotes (if often implicitly) a model of governance at the local and regional levels of the member-states. Primarily through the use of its structural funds, the EU seeks to create incentives for closer public–private cooperation at these institutional levels. More importantly, however, the EU Commission frequently practices multilevel exchanges by corresponding directly with regional and local authorities, thus bypassing the state.

One obvious question, which we have to address, is the utility of an institutional perspective on MLG. There are two general reasons why we believe that perspective is important. First, although policy and political action may be increasingly shaped through informal processes by a multitude of actors at several different institutional levels, formal political institutions still matter a great deal. The institutions matter because they are the undisputed channel between the state and the citizenry in terms of democratic input and accountability. As we argued in Chapter 5, in order for MLG to be democratic, institutions need to play a *primus inter pares* role in MLG (see also Peters and Pierre, 2004). Although regional governments may have a democratic element, the principal, if weak, democratic element of the EU is the linkage to elected governments at the level of the state.

MLG tends to be problem-oriented, bringing together actors centered round a particular policy problem and arguably better equipped at identifying problems than presenting sustainable solutions. However, given their greater continuity and accumulation of professional expertise, institutions tend to be rather skillful in devising solutions, as we discussed in Chapter 4. The combination of their democratic nature and their ability to design solutions to societal problems makes institutions extremely important actors in MLG processes. To be sure, it could even be argued that as governance becomes more fluid and informal, the more important will institutions become. In governance processes where there is a significant variety of actors and where many actors participate on an ad hoc basis, institutions will become critical participants by virtue of their continuity; in a setting where most actors come and go, any actor who is more continuously involved will have a strong position.

Institutional reform and changing intergovernmental relationships

It is interesting to note that much of the development toward MLG has taken place with very few formal, institutional changes within the governments involved in the process. True, a number of countries in Western Europe implemented decentralization reforms during the 1980s and 1990s (Pierre and Peters, 2000; Sharpe, 1988) but at least in some national contexts those reforms were confirmations of a development that was already in progress, and not so much institutional changes aimed at creating new forms of MLG. Thus, much of the decentralization that has taken place in the Scandinavian countries during the past two decades could be seen as an institutional adaptation to the actual modus operandi of these governments. In other cases, such as the creation of new institutions for regional economic development in the UK, institutional reform was implemented primarily in order to strengthen collaborative and concerted action between the public sector and private businesses. It is yet too early to say to what extent these regional institutions will also foster new models of regional governance in Britain, although devolution to Scotland and Wales and discussions of governments for the English regions make those changes more likely.

The local level

Local government is a far more heterogeneous phenomenon than is often realized (see Keating, 1992). The predominant notion of local authorities as weak, fragmented, and almost entirely the captives of the local and regional economic structures is largely explained by the predominance of British and American urbanists—along with the occasional French or Scandinavian contribution—in the academic debate on these issues. Even then, however, one can find examples of local governments that have been successful in carving out their own spheres of autonomy in the face of the seeming dominance of other levels of government.

Interestingly, separating federal states from unitary states is of little help in giving a systematic account of the development of local government. In the UK, local government is typically described as fragmented or "messy" (Leach and Percy-Smith, 2000; Lowndes, forthcoming). Moreover, local authorities in Britain are constitutionally weak with basically no local autonomy guaranteed by the state. In fact, it is the opposite pattern that prevails; according to the ultra vires principle, British local government may only undertake tasks which Parliament allows them to do (Gurr and King, 1987). In the Scandinavian countries, the pattern is exactly the opposite. Here, local autonomy enjoys strong constitutional support, and imposing any limitation on that autonomy is a delicate political project. In fact, the strength of local autonomy in the Scandinavian states is intriguing, given their nature of unitary states; in most such states, regional and local institutions tend to be explicitly subordinate to central government. The British but also the French case could be said to be more typical to the group of unitary states in this respect.

Thus, if central–local relationships in Britain are clearly dominated by central government, intergovernmental relationships in the Scandinavian countries have for a long period of time been characterized by a somewhat paradoxical pattern. On the one hand, the constitutions—as well as the political rhetoric on all levels of government and among all political parties—herald the idea of local autonomy and local self-government. On the other hand, however, local governments (*kommuner*) exercise very little autonomous policy or action when measured as the percentage of their budget over which they have exclusive control. Throughout most of the postwar period, most of the local governments' budgets consist of state grants which they receive for implementing state policies and programs, primarily in education and social welfare. Only a rather minor part of the local governments' financial resources is spent on locally designed programs. Moreover, this part of the local governments' activities comprises most of the least politically salient areas such as culture, leisure, and economic development. So, while the formal local autonomy in these countries is extensive, in real terms it is less impressive.

How has this pattern of intergovernmental relations evolved and how can the discrepancy between the rhetoric of local autonomy on the one hand and the practice of subordination on the other be sustained? In order to get a grip on these questions, we need to look at the historical process which created the current state of affairs. The Scandinavian welfare state is—as many observers have noted (Montin, 1994; Pierre, 1994)—a local welfare state; while overarching policies and programs have been designed at the central government level, the thrust of welfare state service delivery takes place at the regional and local institutional levels. In order to create the necessary institutional vehicles for the expansion of the welfare state, an extensive process of local government modernization began in the 1960s (Strömberg and Westerståhl, 1984). The creation of the bigger and stronger local authorities had a profound impact on the relationship between the state and the local authorities. A less anticipated outcome of the amalgamation process—which has been much more profound in Sweden than in the other Scandinavian countries—was that local authorities now had developed the institutional capacity necessary to resist pressures from central government. With some exaggeration it could be argued that the state had "built the perfect beast"; the new *kommuner* turned out to be more difficult to command and control, compared to the smaller and weaker municipalities.

Across Western Europe, intergovernmental relationships are also strongly affected by changes in the economy. The macroeconomic problems facing the West European states during the 1980s (Sharpe, 1988) helped trigger an extensive political project of decentralization. Such reform had the double blessing of responding to a critique against too centralized government and at the same time allowing the state to "hive off" some financial responsibilities to regional and local government. Furthermore, as the previous cross-national observations suggested, the relationship between institutional levels is also shaped to a considerable degree by the nature of the overarching political project pursued by central government. Welfare state projects tend to rely heavily on the collaboration of local government in the delivery of services. Ensuring such compliance among autonomous local governments has not always been a trivial matter.

The regional level

Institutional reform at the regional level—the proverbial forgotten level of the political system in many unitary states—has been much slower compared to the local level in most countries but gained significant momentum during the 1990s. To some extent, reform was triggered by the EU's focus on regions. However, there was also a need to devise institutional solutions which—as was the objective in some jurisdictions—offer some political and democratic control over economic development and which can help bring together political and corporate actors at the regional levels.

Regional political institutions, particularly in unitary states, have for long been perceived as poorly equipped to mobilize the principal actors within their regional territory toward joint, concerted action that could boost the regional economy. In order to ameliorate this perceived deficiency, central government in several of the West European countries have launched programs intended to recreate the regions as an economic space and to strengthen the regional institutions (Evans and Harding, 1997; but see Wright, 1998). It would, however, be severely misleading to underestimate the role of the EU and its commitment to a "Europe of the Regions" as the key force propelling this development. Similarly, although regional institutional reform seems to be in vogue these days, there is significant uncertainty about how to design these institutions. As Peter Newman (2000) aptly puts it, "regional reform remains on the agenda in most European states and nowhere is there the feeling that that the institutional mixture is about right." To some extent, this uncertainty is probably caused by a similar confusion as regards what should be the role of those institutions.

These institutional changes have, not very surprisingly, played out quite differently in different national contexts. In Germany, strong regions were already in place and probably helped the German regions to capitalize on the EU's initiatives. In France, economically defined regions existed in some parts of the country but their number and cohesion increased quickly as the structural funds emerged as a major source of potential funding for regional initiatives. The UK followed suit, creating eight regions for economic development. This elaboration of the institutional structure represents to some extent institutional isomorphism (Dimaggio and Powell, 1991), with the institutions of government adapting to the nature of the economy they were intended to regulate and to support.

Sweden too has been experimenting with institutional change at the regional level, for example, in the Gothenburg region. A large-scale experiment is currently being implemented, in order to devise appropriate institutions aiming at boosting regional economic development and also to bring this process under some form of political control. Stated in a slightly different language, it is a project aiming at creating effective regional, political, and economic governance. A key element of the reform is to produce so-called regional growth agreements (RGA) (in Swedish *regionala tillväxtavtal*). The general idea behind the RGA reform has been to lump together all the various specific grants coming from central government to the regions—grants for regional economic development, environmental protection, some education programs, labor-market programs, culture, nature preservation projects, and so on—into one block grant. The regions would then be permitted to spend that grant according to a program which had been negotiated among political institutions at the regional and local levels, the business community, organized interests, voluntary associations, and so on. Also, private businesses were encouraged not just to participate in the process of deliberating the RGAs but also to put their money where their proverbial mouths were, that is, to make contributions toward the financing of the projects.

Central government reserved the right to approve formally the RGAs before the projects listed in the agreement were given funding, indicating that some hierarchy remained in the process. Still, the RGA program remains a textbook example of central government creating incentives to build systems of governance at the regional level and devolving some powers to that governance arrangement. It could well be that the Swedish political system in these regions is now transitioning from a reasonably hierarchical system toward one which is more similar to what Reigner (2001) calls "coadministration" that has been evolving within the French system. This system features shared responsibilities for programs and a division of labor between different institutional levels, rather than formal command and control. Clearly if a system that has been as hierarchical as the French (but see Gremion, 1976) can make this transformation then more devolved systems certainly should be able to do so.

Changing intergovernmental relationships

Are these new, emerging intergovernmental relationships—which play out differently in different national settings, as pointed out earlier—typical to MLG? Well, yes and no. Yes, in so far as institutional relationships in countries such as the Scandinavian states, Australia (Painter, 2001) and France (Reigner, 2001) are becoming increasingly negotiated and also in so far as the growing number of institutional levels is concerned. Overall, there appears to be a tendency in intergovernmental relationships to move from hierarchical control and toward a negotiated division of labor among the levels. The relaxation of state rules and legislation in many core state sectors testifies to a strategy aiming at granting regional and local authorities a more immediate responsibility for these programs. That shift in responsibility at the same time allows for greater variation in public service among regions and locales. Again, there are exceptions to this pattern; Britain would be one such example, apart from the devolution projects in Scotland and Wales and the newly created economic development regions, central government control remains the defining feature of intergovernmental relationships. Overall, however, the heyday of achieving an equal standard as the key objective in public service provision is clearly gone. Instead, the current emphasis is on adapting public service to local needs and local demand; to allow local service providers to "tailor" their services according to clients' preferences; and to open up for customer choice.

By dislocating political control downward and outward in the political system (please note that we are not discussing the extensive upward dislocation of political control to the EU), the state attains two important goals. First, it defines clearer roles for institutions at all levels and accords them more autonomy to specialize in that role. Thus, for example, institutions operating under market, or quasi-market, conditions can develop their corporate, profit-making nature more effectively if they are allowed more discretion from the political echelons of government. Other institutions can use their autonomy to engage in closer cooperation with key actors in their external environments. Second, central government can focus on its traditional role of policy making, coordination, implementation, and so on (Pierre and Peters, 2000). It is, however, important to recognize that these displacements of power and control do not automatically signal the impending decline of the state. It is an alteration of the division of power within the political system initiated by the state, and the state retains the capability to reassess that order if and when it so chooses.

Thus, the development we can observe in intergovernmental relationships is perhaps not so much typical to MLG as it is of the evolving policy style and role of the state in society more broadly. It represents a development toward governance functioning at different institutional levels more than a governance arrangement negotiated between or among those levels. A good deal of the activity of governance remains confined to one level or another, with the relationships remaining almost as formal as those of more traditional and constitutional federalism. Let us now turn to the final part of the chapter and discuss how the changes described earlier have affected the process of policy implementation.

Policy implementation in a multilevel governance context

As we can see, there exists an interesting correlation between the nature of the overarching political projects that states pursue and the institutional strength that characterizes these states at different points in time. Another fairly clear pattern, looking at developments of state strength over time, is that the institutional capabilities of West European states are to a very large extent determined by the states themselves and not by exogenous forces like the market or transnational institutions. Certainly, we can point at several developments which have undermined some of the historical strength of these states. But these reforms, we need to remind ourselves, were initiated and implemented by the states themselves. The growing strength of the EU, or the deregulation of financial markets which was a precondition for the emergence of a global economy, were both state-driven reforms.

This, needless to say, is not very far from a classical institutional argument; states develop the institutional arrangements necessary to pursue the dominant political projects at any particular time. The institutional setup of the laissez-faire state was different from that of the typical welfare state which, in turn, was different from that of a developmental state (Johnson, 1982; Okimoto, 1988). That said, institutionalists also emphasize the longevity of institutions and the inertia in institutional change. It could well be that the West European states during the past decade or so are cases of states undergoing a process of change from an interventionist toward an enabling regime. The increasing focus on macroeconomic balance and low inflation has pushed states to cut back on public expenditures and to adopt a policy style which is considerably less dirigiste compared to the early 1980s. But the institutional structures of the state still bear some resemblance with the bigger, redistributive states which were typical of the early postwar period. Bert Rockman has described the present situation in which we see big governments in small states in many of the advanced industrial democracies (Rockman, 1998).

The Swedish case would fit this description rather well. As argued earlier, we can identify a reasonably high degree of correspondence between institutional change, intergovernmental relationships, and public service objectives in the governance process. This correspondence also applies to the role of subnational government in policy implementation; when policies were interventionist and emphasized equality across the country, intergovernmental relationships were clearly hierarchical. As the policy style has changed toward one more of bargaining that permits some territorial differentiation of policy, so too have the intergovernmental relationships. These relationships now more closely approximate equality than hierarchy.

Institutional reform at the regional levels paints a similar picture. Although these reforms have yet to find their final form, it appears clear that by encouraging a development toward governance, the state has devised regional structures which it is quite likely to experience increasing problems with controlling in the future. At both levels institutional reform has set in train processes of adaptive behavior among key actors—for instance, the creation of new networks or coalitions, increasing cooperation between political and corporate actors, or strategies of positioning the city or region in the international arena—which tend to strengthen the political capabilities at these levels, something which, in turn, makes them more difficult to control by the state.

Taken together, these patterns of institutional change and the growing emphasis on governance at the local and regional levels have had profound effects on the role that regional and local government are capable of playing in the implementation of public policy. Regional and local institutions now play substantially different roles in implementation because the objectives and design of many policies have changed. Especially for economic policy, the prevailing pattern has shifted away from a rather strict top-down, interventionist policy toward less targeted programs aimed at enabling private businesses to prosper, and to have greater latitude in shaping their own business environment.

The only significant development that seems to question the logical relationship between institutional change, intergovernmental relationships, and policy style relates to the long-term effects of the emergence of governance at the regional and local levels. While intergovernmental relationships in a constitutional perspective could be conceived of as a zero-sum game—one level's increase in power and control is at the expense of the other levels—the governance perspective highlights the extent to which institutions at different levels can enhance their ability to steer and coordinate their territory through their involvement with other levels, or perhaps with the civil society. Thus, governance, from that perspective could be described as an empowerment of institutions, not in relationship to each other but in relationship to their external environment (Pierre and Peters, 2000).

By creating incentives for the development of such governance structures, central government has probably contributed to strengthening political institutions at the regional and local levels. We have previously argued that an important unintended consequence of that development could well be that regional and local authorities become more autonomous and assertive vis-à-vis central government. Thus, shifting the perspective from government to governance, in the real world as well as in academic discussions, in the end will strengthen one set of institutions in ways that might not have been anticipated.

7
Governance, Accountability, and Democratic Legitimacy

The past decade or so has witnessed an extensive debate concerning what is believed to be important changes in the processes and instruments with which the contemporary state governs society. As we discussed in Chapter 2, the debate features a wide range of different theories and perspectives on governance and the role of government in that process (Pierre, 2000). One of the main issues has been the capacity of the state to govern society in an era when the state is cutting back at the same time as the external environment of the state is becoming increasingly complex. Alongside this discussion there has also been a debate on how to conceptualize and understand the new forms of governance we have seen emerge during the 1980s and 1990s (Pierre, 2000).

The analysis in Chapter 2 substantiated the many different roles of the state and how these roles relate to the overarching function of the state to govern society. This wide range of different roles played by the state in contemporary society is worth noticing. Dismissing the state as the center of governing capacity within society is a very bold assertion indeed. To be sure, the debate itself to some extent begs the question of how theories are formed and what empirical evidence is employed to sustain the theory. We believe that the conception of the state as a marginalized structure in society is greatly exaggerated. This stateless model of governance has its roots primarily in accounts of changes in the British state toward developing new and "softer," that is, less obtrusive and interventionist policy instruments; toward opening up new channels for exchange with actors in the external environment of the public sector; and toward a policy style which is less interventionist and more market-embracing compared to the policy style of the 1960s and 1970s (see Kooiman, 1993, 2003). Given their grounding in British and other Westminster systems, the scholars involved often failed to note that many other societies had been governed in this "softer" way for decades (Heisler, 1974; Kraemer, 1968).

The theory claims, sometimes explicitly and sometimes implicitly, to be a means of resolving complex problems of governing in a range of problems, but the discussion is often confused. The debate among governance scholars is probably caused by the slippery nature of the concept of governance. We have in a previous context spent some energy on a conceptual analysis of governance (Pierre and Peters, 2000). Also, Chapter 2 represents an attempt to take that discussion one step further by introducing a framework toward an understanding of the state–society dimension of governance. The governance debate so far has been a slightly confusing sequel to the interest among political scientists during the late 1980s and 1990s in "bringing the state back in." In retrospect it appears as if parts of the governance debate have attempted to move the state back *out* of governing into the relative oblivion it found itself during the heyday of the "behavioral revolution." (Almond, 1988; March and Olsen, 1989). We believe this movement to be unfortunate, simply because it is an implicit argument that the state has lost political leverage. This may have occurred to the extent that is sometimes suggested appears counterintuitive if not empirically speaking incorrect (see Mann, 1997). A more realistic and intriguing approach to the role of the state in contemporary governance appears to be how the state is transforming to adapt both to globalization and to the new and lower profile it tends to assume domestically.

In order to understand that process of change, this chapter traces different ideas concerning the centrality of the state over the past several decades. By revisiting the debate on state–society relationships that occurred during the 1980s and 1990s we believe that we can outline a more realistic trajectory of how the debate on these issues has changed and what has been believed to be the key governance problems in different political and institutional contexts. We also believe that this avenue of analysis can be extremely rewarding for coming to grips with what is causing the current problems with accountability and legitimacy of the state and public policy. The issues are hardly new ones but the nature of the debate has been changing significantly.

Also, it is important to differentiate between the rather negative "hollow" conception of the state and the more positive "enabling" conception. The former, hollow conception assumes that government has become incapable of governing, that its center and its very purpose have been hollowed out (Weller *et al.*, 1997). As already noted, this characterization of change may be based largely on a Westminster conception that, despite some claims of having no conception of the state as in Continental political philosophy, has depended very much on a strong, centralized state as the source of governance. The enabling conception, on the other hand, is more Scandinavian and assumes that the state remains a crucial actor but that its role has shifted to be one of mobilizing governance resources from a number of sources in order to provide direction and service to society in ways that might not be possible without coordination through that "central mind of government."[1]

One change in the debate has been an increased emphasis on the familiar, yet crucial, question of accountability (see Aucoin and Heintzman, 2002) and with it the legitimacy of the public sector and its activities. As we discuss in greater detail later, a number of attempts at reforming existing state structures and procedures have altered the possibilities for making accountability, as we have known it, function effectively. This change in the accountability regime is already operating, but remains poorly conceptualized. This paucity of conceptualization appears true both in the academic literature and in the practice of government. For example, although contracts have come to be used increasingly as a means of delivering public services, the means necessary for holding contractors accountable are often not developed adequately (Peters, 2000d).

The basic argument in this chapter is that an understanding of the contemporary accountability and legitimacy problematic requires a departure from the political and institutional logic that has characterized the liberal-democratic state. For all of its flaws and problems, that liberal model of governing provided at a minimum a reasonably clear institutional linkage between elected officials, public policies, and the electorate. Holding elected officials of an "enabling state" to account is, democratically speaking, not a very satisfactory arrangement. Similarly, a performance-related model of *political* accountability has yet to be formulated; the list of unsettled incidents of public service errors which has not been politically resolved is already extensive (see, for instance, Barberis, 1998; Mulgan, 2000; Polidano, 1997; Thomas, 1998) and there is little reason to believe that the NPM school of public service production will come up with a satisfactory answer to these problems.

As we review the debate on these issues that has occurred over the past couple of decades, we find that the shift from government to governance as the key process through which collective goals are defined and pursued highlights performance taking precedence over accountability, especially accountability defined through means of political institutions. A few decades ago, the main concern of constitutional architects was how the state could be capable of governing society, when the pressures from the surrounding society appeared to "overload" the state with demands and ever-growing expectations. This situation triggered a search for means through which to enhance the overall performance of the state, a search that, in turn, served as a powerful motivation for bringing private sector concepts and models of service production into the public sector.

What was lost as one unintended consequence of the reform process was, to a considerable degree, accountability for actions by the state, or more exactly for the actions of agents of the state. The new, increasingly predominant, paradigm of public sector management is based on several concepts that tend to minimize accountability. For example, managerial autonomy and market-based accountability as a function of customer choice (Barberis, 1998; Hood, 1991; Peters, 2001a) are central to NPM and both minimize conventional forms of political accountability. The problem of ensuring accountability of career public servants with the devaluing of politicians in these models and the empowerment of managers was never properly resolved. If anything, the continuing displacement of power and the enforced separation of power and responsibility seem to exacerbate the problem.

Moreover, we argue that some form of accountability is a prerequisite for the legitimacy of a democratic government. Political decisions and actions become legitimate if they are made, or at least formally enacted, by elected officials, and those officials must be subject to some form of accountability, whether internal to government or external through the electoral process. By the same token, irregularities in public service delivery can be indirectly resolved through institutionalized channels as long as politicians exercise some degree of control over the public administration. When that political control is relaxed, the legitimacy of the public sector becomes more a matter of its performance; input control. Further, in that context political accountability could be argued to have been replaced by different types of output-related mechanisms of accountability that may have some element of automaticity rather than judgment. The key question is how such a version of accountability can support the legitimacy of elected government.

The chapter initially rehearses the debates on "overloaded government" (Birch, 1984) and the "ungovernability" of society (Crozier *et al.*, 1975) that were influential several decades ago but still have some relevance for understanding questions of governing. We then look at the New Right political ideology and NPM in the context of ideological frameworks and strategies employed to resolve the problems of overload and accountability. Here, we can identify governance as the third link in the chain of reform attempting at resolving problems of overload and ungovernability. Although the ultimate goal of these three strategies of reform is rather similar—lowering the expectations on the state, exploring alternative sources of service delivery, and downplaying the centrality of the state in society—these are three distinctly different models, as we see later. Following this analysis we develop the argument that all three models are unclear with regard to accountability, something which, in turn, raises questions about the legitimacy of the three models of governing.

Overload, ungovernability, and governance

We now proceed to discuss a variety of challenges to governing that have been identified and discussed, as capitalist societies have encountered shifts in their apparent capacity to govern and to survive economically. Despite the apparent successes of most of these governments, when compared to governments in most of the rest of the world, the governments in the advanced industrial democracies were perceived by many citizens to be ineffective and even illegitimate. These governments were deemed to be failing, despite their successes in creating and managing the welfare state, the management of unprecedented economic successes, and a period of relative international peace.

Overloaded government

The general idea in the "overload" literature is that government becomes unable to respond to all demands and expectations placed on it by the public, organized interests, or other actors in the external environment of the state. Such an overload of functions, in turn, undermines the legitimacy of the government. Thus, here is a clear hypothesis for the relationship between efficiency and legitimacy (Dahrendorf, 1960). The legitimacy of the state is sustained not just by democratic constitutional arrangements and politically responsive government, as liberal-democratic theory argues, but also, broadly defined, on the ability of government to keep the public satisfied. In contemporary language, the performance of government means a great deal in how the public views it. "Performance" in this particular context refers not only to public service quality but also, and more importantly, the ability of the state to respond appropriately to demands, to resolve political conflict and produce consent, to define political goals and objectives, and to pursue those goals.

To some extent, the concept of "overloaded" government echoes the political system analysis of the 1960s and 1970s (see, for instance, Easton, 1965). In this theoretical perspective, "overloaded government" is the result of societal demands exceeding the problem-solving capacity of government. It is interesting to revisit this literature because it describes rather aptly problems which since have risen to the forefront of political analysis and administrative reform:

> Every political system must have some finite capacity with respect to the number of demands it can accept for processing into decisions or consider as possible basis of choice. It will have only some finite amount of time available to devote to settling differences politically . . . what we may designate as *demand input overload* could be said to describe a system if, within a specified time interval, the number of demands exceeded an empirically determinable limit. (Easton, 1965:58; italics in original)

Obviously, overload can be caused either by an increasing number of demands on the state, or on a decreasing capacity of the state to respond to address and respond to demands, or because the "gatekeepers" fail to keep demands at a sufficiently low level to allow the political system to process those demands. For systems theorists, organized interests and political parties were key "gatekeeping" structures; however, with the emergence of populist parties (Taggart, 1996) and also interest organizations more concerned with the pursuit of narrowly defined interests than assuming societal responsibilities, these gatekeepers may in fact exacerbate the problem of massive input instead of reducing the flow of demands into government.

Moreover, overload is to some extent a consequence of the state's own actions, and the state's own successes. The expansion of the political sphere in society that characterized Western Europe through the 1960s and 1970s involved rising expectation for the state as a provider of goods and services for the public. Somewhat ironically, perhaps, the relative success of the state as a mediator of social conflict and, more generally, as a governing body, triggered further expectations. These included demands for more distributive and redistributive programs, and for regulation as a means of promoting collective interests in a wide variety of policy sectors. In many countries in Western Europe, the policy style of resolving socioeconomic problems by permitting greater public sector control and/or funding generated massive expectations for similar state actions in an ever large number of additional sectors.

Time seems to have caught up with this academic debate or, more correctly, overload seems to have reemerged as a problem for the state during the 1990s. The decreasing "policy capacity" of many contemporary states increases the risk of overload because the state must, to a growing extent, commission policy advice from external sources. This use of external advice is both tedious for individuals in government and also associated with considerable uncertainties about the quality and direction of the advice (Boston, 1994). Thus, the rather dramatic cutbacks in policy advice capacity throughout the Western world have, in fact, not reduced the risk of overload but exactly the opposite. By putting greater trust either in the market as a problem solver and—as Reagan, Thatcher, and other political leaders with a market-based philosophy chose to do—to try and persuade the public that they should not look to government for help but rather look to themselves to solve problems—governments have tried to alleviate themselves from demands, pressures, and expectations from society.

Thus, overload can be caused by factors and developments outside state control, but it may also be the unintended result of the state's decreasing policy capacity, or, indeed, its success in delivering programs and services which in turn lead the public to ask for more of the same. Indeed, many of the governance problems of the 1960s and 1970s were a product of hubris by the political and administrative elites rather than demands coming from the society. Those elites believed that they had found a solution for many of the problems of the society and the economy and were more than willing to wield that newfound knowledge.

The "ungovernable" society

If overload has been a characteristic of the state, ungovernability primarily has been a feature of society. However, overload and ungovernability both denote a situation in which some kind of imbalance exists between state and society in terms of policy capacity and societal demands. Further, as already noted, the increased complexity of contemporary societies has made governance more difficult, both in terms of the number of demands being advanced and the number of interconnections that must be managed. With respect to the ungovernability problem, it is fair to argue that it is primarily a quality of society more than of the state, so that even the most capable political system may be incapable of ruling effectively with other than Draconian means.[2] Ungovernability may, of course, be in part perceptual as some political systems will attempt to impose greater levels of uniformity on society than will others.

"Ungovernability" is caused, first and foremost, by the growing complexity of society. Kooiman's "societal governance" (Kooiman, 1993) departs from an image of society as so complex that it has become virtually impossible for the state to bring order and a common direction into it. The state itself is embedded in a nonhierarchical, multitier institutional system where negotiation has replaced previous patterns of steering and control. The market, too, is becoming increasingly characterized by a global economy penetrating domestic (national and local) economies, creating greater volatility and unpredictability. If the more interventionist policy style of the 1960s and 1970s had the important advantage of making the economy slightly more predictable for the state, the deregulation and less obtrusive macroeconomic style of the 1980s and 1990s has both reduced the number of points of contact between the state and the market and allowed the economy to develop more according to its own logic.

Both of these factors have contributed to making the economy less predictable and less governable.

Furthermore, across the Western world, we see declining trust in political institutions and a declining party membership; developments which together suggest that the legitimacy of the political system of the twentieth century seems to be less stable compared to a couple of decades ago. Society is thus becoming increasingly complex, incoherent, and unpredictable at the same time as the traditional pillars of government appear to be losing their grip over political representation and decision making. Governability is to some degree not just a matter of society's complexity; it is also about the state's leverage over society and about the legitimacy of those levers and the institutions controlling them. Further, social institutions themselves may be in decline, as evidenced in the large debate over the nature of social capital in a range of countries (Putnam *et al.*, 1993).

To some extent, the notion of ungovernability as a fairly recent phenomenon exaggerates the governability of society—and the capacity of the state to govern—in times past. Ungovernability appears rather to have become a problem at the confluence of two developments. One of these developments saw the state take on a higher profile in society, as was the case in the 1960s and 1970s both in the US and the countries of Western Europe. The other development affecting the governability of society was the increasing complexity of those societies, the loss of cohesion and homogeneity, and increasing tensions brought about by an increasingly zero-sum economy in many.

A slightly different version of the ungovernability argument can be found in the now large literature on networks. Several observers argue that the governance of the modern state occurs primary at the level of the policy sector where cohesive and powerful "policy networks" effectively control the sector. Indeed, these networks are sometimes sufficiently powerful to resist policy changes initiated by government and political institutions (Marsh and Rhodes, 1992a; Rhodes, 1997). In addition, administrative reforms over the past several decades have exacerbated this problem by extolling the need to empower both senior managers and lower echelon workers in organizations, as well as ascribing more rights to the recipients of government benefits. From the vantage point of the government (taken as an entity), this lack of coordination and coherence clearly represents a case of ungovernability.

As is the case with overload, ungovernability is—albeit to a lesser extent than was the case with overload—to some extent, directly or indirectly, caused by the state itself. Certainly, the growing complexity of society cannot be said to be a deliberate consequence of public policy. However, if governability denotes some kind of "equilibrium" existing between society's complexity on the one hand and the policy capacity of governments on the other, then it appears fair to say that the dismantling, or at least minimizing of the policy capacity which we have been witnessing across the Western world over the past couple of decades (Peters, 2001a; Peters and Savoie, 1998) has contributed to the exacerbated governing, and governability, problems we have encountered in many cases.

Governance as a solution

The dual, and intertwined, problems of government overload and the ungovernability of society generated a variety of responses from the public sector. Some of those responses have been political and ideological, including the rather extreme reactions expressed through Thatcherism and Reaganism (Savoie, 1994). The assumptions motivating these political responses were that government had assumed responsibilities that it could not easily fulfill and had, in the process, undermined their own legitimacy as well as undermining the capacity of other socioeconomic structures—most obviously the market—to operate effectively to solve human needs. Further, it was argued that the more intrusive public sector undermined the capacity of the Third Sector to play the strong role of which it might be capable if the more intrusive state were less active.

Other approaches to reducing or eliminating these problems have been more technical and managerial. For example, the spread of the ideas associated with the NPM may be seen as, at least in part, a reaction to perceived failures in governance, and the associated desire to make government perform more efficiently (Pollitt and Bouckaert, 2000). Performance management is one of the central features of the most recent round of reforms, with budgets and other allocations becoming dependent upon the assessment of their performance (Bouckaert and Halachmi, 1995). These mechanisms tend to introduce one form of accountability into the central allocative processes of government and to create a potentially mechanistic conception of what governing means.

The above two reactions to problems in governing represent two alternative mechanisms for coping with problems of overload and ungovernability. On the one hand, government can cope with overload by shedding some of the load; the obvious reaction of Reagan, Thatcher, and other members of the New Right. In any number of countries, governments have eliminated activities, privatized state-owned firms, and sought to reduce a range of obligations of the public sector. This strategy often was less successful than its advocates thought it might be, given that many programs had powerful constituencies inside and outside government and further many programs were entitlements that were difficult for any government to terminate. Thus, despite their commitments to the contrary, public spending actually increased in both the absolute and relative sense, during the administrations of those paragons of conservative virtue.

In addition to the problem of entitlements encountered by would-be reducers of overload, the obvious political difficulty in this approach to coping with problems of governance is that the public may be somewhat schizophrenic about the "load" of public sector activities. In most cases the public want their services continued but resist pay for those services through taxation. When we examine the range of public opinion data taken over the past several decades this inconsistency of views becomes very apparent (Newton and Kaase, 1996; Peters, 1991:ch. 6). Citizens want few if any reductions in public services, and in many cases want to have the services expanded. At the same time, the public argue that taxes are too high and they want to pay less for what they get for government.

Another significant approach to those two problems has been to make public programs perform better and more efficiently, and to eliminate at least a part of the total costs of governing by reducing the costs of each service being delivered to citizens. This is one potential way of squaring the circle of a public that demands more service for less money. The NPM has, among its other attributes, a self-proclaimed capacity to make the public sector organizations function more efficiently. So, for example, instilling greater competition into government—in both the structures for delivering policy and the management of personnel—is assumed to be able to provide the same services to the public at less direct costs in taxes to the public.

Like reducing programs to save money, the NPM may not be an undivided benefit for the public, and generates problems for effective governing. For example, the disaggregation of the public sector implied by the concepts of the NPM creates significant problems of coordination and coherence. In addition, the autonomy granted to actors within the public sector can limit the accountability of public programs, and with that the capacity of elected officials to control the actions of bureaucracies and other public sector entities. These changes, and other types of reforms associated with this range of ideas, have now created the need to introduce yet further reforms to the public sector, many directed at enhancing accountability.

Governance as the other solution

The two earlier reactions to problems of governing certainly had some benefits for society and for government, but also carried with them some major problems. The two prior reactions to problems produced responses that made the process of governing less directly connected to political responsibility but at the same time also began to introduce new standards by which to judge the activities of governments. This involved shifting from a strictly political internal conception of accountability to a more external and performance-based conception of accountability. The virtue of the latter is that it focuses on what government organizations do on a day-to-day basis, rather than attempting to discover spectacular failures that could embarrass a government. Still, divorcing representative political institutions and procedures from the accountability debate does present some problems for democratic conceptions of government.

Governance and accountability

Accountability has become a key problem in contemporary governance, primarily for three reasons. First, unlike statecraft within the liberal-democratic state, governance is primarily about processes and dynamics; while political institutions are an important aspect of governance, the emphasis in governance is clearly on processes rather than institutions. Governance today frequently includes a wide variety of actors such as public–private partnerships, voluntary associations, private businesses, political institutions existing at different levels of government, and so on. Governance is about developing processes through which those actors can cooperate in order to govern the society and do so in a more democratic and inclusive manner than might be possible in conventional state-centric conceptualizations (and practices) of governing.

Some of these actors—most of the political actors—can be held to account through the election process (leaving aside for a moment the perennial problem of bureaucratic accountability (Gruber, 1992) but most of them cannot. True, the problem of allowing nonelected actors access to the policy-making process is not in any way new— we need only think of the corporatist states—but that having been said, governance poses a real problem in terms of accountability. The advocates of NPM argue that governance in fact has a more immediate and visible system of accountability than the liberal-democratic state because customer choice sends clear and direct signals on customer preferences. Accountability, then, becomes almost exclusively a performance-related problem. NPM supporters also point at stake-holderism as an alternative model of accountability in governance.

The problem with these models of accountability is that they only look at one aspect of what governments do, that is, public service delivery, and ignore the other important sector of government activity, namely, the exercise of legitimate political power. Furthermore, these models of governing are far from traditional notions of party government, where the idea was that it was political parties as collectivities that were responsible (and responsive) more than individual elected officials. The key problem in all of this change in modes of governing is that we still have not developed a model of *political* accountability in a governance perspective. The focus on process is one problem for governing; the focus on performance (and service to the public) is another.

Second, governance has emerged as an important perspective because it concentrates on performance, both in terms of public services and in terms of finding alternative ways and political resources for the state to maintain some steering capacity. While governance should not be confused with NPM (see Peters and Pierre, 1998), both strands of thought emphasize the importance of performance, and both also recognize the need to identify the basis of governing for the individual citizen/consumer. In the NPM (see Pollitt and Bouckaert, 2000) the emphasis is on the performance of individual civil servants and/or their organizations, with little or no concern about the cumulation of that performance, or indeed about its integration across the range of interconnected organizations within the public sector (see Peters, 2001a:ch. 6). One of the consequences of the emphasis on individual organizations and managers appears to be an increasing incoherence in policies and actions within government, and hence paradoxically greater difficulties in creating effective governance for the public as a whole.

The third problem, finally, relates to the emerging image of the state in governance as "the enabling state." This term is to a great extent an adequate description of the image that state actors in many national contexts are attempting to "sell" to their publics. The state today is engaged in less rowing and more steering, to quote Osborne and Gaebler (1991); the state now attempts to capitalize on, and to coordinate, resources controlled by a wide variety of actors, and to employ those resources in the pursuit of collective goals for the society. Again, we must ask where this version of the state leaves the concept of accountability for the state. For example, the state may be successful in its role of "enabling" other actors that possess resources necessary for governance, that is, if the state provides ideal preconditions for the corporate sector. These actors, however, may turn out to perform inadequately, but who is to be held accountable for that policy failure?[3] Economic development is a top political priority for most governments today and we have observed huge efforts being made at removing what is believed to impair economic growth, not least regulatory frameworks. But who is to be held to account if such enabling measures do not help stimulate growth? As Claus Offe pointed out quite some time ago, private capital's option *not* to act in accordance with incentives provided by political institutions is an important source of its political influence over government (Offe, 1985). Placed in the context of the accountability of the enabling state, this type of influence becomes all the more important as the very nature of this form of governing is dependent upon the involvement of nonstate actors. These influences are all the more relevant as the range of actors having influence through the threat of nonparticipation increases.

Governance and legitimacy

One of the key differences between the "overload" and "governability" debates on the one hand, and the contemporary governance debate on the other, revolves around the issue of legitimacy and accountability. In the earlier debates about the capacity of the public sector to perform its tasks adequately, legitimacy was identified as a problem because the state appeared to be incapable of accommodating the expectations placed upon it, either in terms of appropriately processing inputs from society, or in terms of producing effective programs and policies. This perspective is clearly a political approach to the question of legitimacy, with the assumption that if the appropriate political processes are followed then legitimacy could be established. At an intermediate level, there are symbolic elements to the adoption and implementation of programs, so that merely pursuing certain types of programs may enhance the legitimacy of a sitting government, whether the programs of the government are in fact effective or not.

From the governance perspective, however, legitimacy emerges as a problem because the state is under-performing. The raison d'etre and legitimacy of the state in a governance perspective is derived primarily from its performance in terms of outputs—services, decisions, and actions. There are, however, still some important questions about procedures and democratic capacity in the contemporary discussion of the state. For example, movements such as communitarianism (Etzioni, 1995) and deliberative democracy (Hunold, 2001) point to the need to make government democratic, open and transparent, as well as effective. The governance emphasis may tend to bureaucratize the practice of democracy, with a good deal of public participation now being directed toward the bureaucracy. Further, even more than with the corporatism characterizing much of the political discussion of the 1970s and 1980s, social groups have come to be considered essential to the functioning of the state.

It is not only in theory that there has been a continued concern with the democratic performance of government, so that the general public and political elites have both raised questions about the means of ensuring and enhancing democracy in contemporary political systems. For example, governance within the EU has long generated questions about the "democratic deficit" and the proposed expansion of the Union that may make the system even more remote;[4] this is one of the many problems of democracy that arise in systems of MLG. Also, the need to dismantle many aspects of the welfare state has tended to make many citizens question the capacity of governments to govern in a manner that responds to the demands of the public.[5]

While the emphasis on performance in contemporary governance theory has not entirely excluded the concern with democracy and participation, that concern with performance is not itself entirely novel either. For example, the by now rather dated literature on political development had one strand that stressed the connection between legitimacy and effectiveness (Huntington, 1966; Lipset, 1959). Further, the extensive literature in political science on public policy that began to be developed at about the same time tended to equate the capacity to make and implement policies effectively with the success of the political system (Mitchell and Mitchell, 1969). Indeed, a good deal of the public administration literature (implementation for example) has been concerned with the effectiveness of public organizations, as well as with their adherence to procedural and legal criterion of appropriate behavior. By no means does this discussion imply that the strong emphasis on state performance in governance is not significant, but rather it points to the extent to which we are dealing with relative emphases in theory rather than sharp, absolute breaks with the past.

The approach to governing contained within governance theory represents—to reiterate a point made earlier—a significant difference compared to the liberal-democratic state model described earlier, where legitimacy rests primarily with the state's ability to produce consent. That is, the success of the state in the liberal-democratic process of governing depends primarily upon its political performance or the ability of constitutional frameworks to provide elected political leadership reflecting popular opinions and preference (what we might call legalistic performance). That model of governing demands that political elites be open to political pressures and demands and attempt to incorporate them into the governing process, but does not appear to imply a direct one-to-one correspondence between demands and their decisions. Other approaches to governing (again practical as well as theoretical) generated prior to the contemporary concern with governance did attempt to link inputs and outputs. Corporatism, for example, was a reaction to governing in the liberal-democratic style, and assumed a close linkage between the demands placed upon government and the decisions that are made, even if the source of those demands was relatively restricted.

Again, however, we should be careful not to overemphasize the differences between the governance models and the liberal-democratic model. Certainly there was a concern with policies among both citizens and elites in the liberal-democratic state, but the principal source of legitimacy was procedural. Even if government policies were ill conceived and went wrong, as they certainly did any number of times, the mechanisms for coping with those failures were more primarily political and remained internal to state institutions to a greater extent than might be true for the contemporary "enabling state." In the latter style of governing, the accountability for policy failures would have to be shared rather widely among state and nonstate actors, with the concomitant problems of assigning responsibility and then providing some means of enforcing accountability for actions. The problem of "many hands," as well as that of "dirty hands" is endemic in public life, and is becoming exacerbated by movement toward the "enabling state" style of governance, in which the central actors are mobilizers and honest brokers as much as they are the wielders of authority. In a democracy, however, accountability is meant to be commensurate with authority.

Conclusion

This chapter has examined the changing nature of government and governance in the contemporary world influenced by globalization, declining public confidence in almost all social and political institutions, and growing adherence to neoliberal political ideologies. These environmental changes have obvious consequences for governments and their capacity to generate compliance from the public. One of the characterizations of these problems was the ungovernability of society, while another was that governments were overloaded with problems and expectations. In both instances traditional means of influencing the society appeared to have exhausted their utility.

Governments have not been totally quiescent and have developed their own strategies for coping with these forces limiting their governing capacity. Some of those strategies involved a virtual denial of the role of the state, assuming that the market and society are more suited to providing goods and services than are governments. Other strategies involved making government perform better the tasks that it had undertaken, assuming that if those services could be provided at lower cost and in a less "bureaucratic" manner then the public would accept them more readily. Both of these strategies experienced some successes, but also created a range of new problems in the process.

A third strategy has become more popular. Generally parading under the banner of governance, this approach to steering society emphasizes just that—steering. As such it does not imply the more direct imposition of control from above characteristic of more traditional forms of ruling, but rather depends upon mobilizing, organizing, and enabling resources available in all segments of the political economy. While in many ways also successful, governance approaches have other problems, most notably difficulties in isolating and enforcing accountability. Thus, merely advocating that state and society should be more supportive of one another may only be a beginning toward understanding and then redesigning patterns of governing that are at once efficient and democratic.

8
Conclusion: Governance and Political Power

Governance is, as we have been arguing throughout, the process of making and implementing collective decisions for a society. We have also been arguing that, although the governance debate involves a number of questions about the role of social actors in that process, government remains a central, if not the central actor, in the process. We do not say this simply because we are terribly old-fashioned neanderthals who will not admit that the world has changed. We know very well that the world of governing has changed, but there are empirical and normative realities that make us believe that we need to understand the institutions of government if we are to understand governance in a democratic society.

In some ways a focus on institutions could appear misleading. After all, governance is typically conceived of as an inclusive process transgressing the border between public and private in society. Also, governance for many observers has become important as a result of growing societal complexities and the purported inability of institutions to handle these new contingencies. To some, sticking to an institutional perspective on governance could appear to be a rather pointless exercise in trying to put Humpty Dumpty together again.

However, there are plenty of important arguments to defend this view on governance. A political analysis of governance cannot be confined to pursue what would be the most efficient coordination of actors, or what would be the optimal blend of resources from different actors or interests. For political scientists, values such as efficiency and effectiveness must be weighed against values like legitimacy and democracy. Efficient governance arrangements that do not allow for

133

some degree of democratic transparency and control can never be sustainable in the longer term.

Furthermore, while we all acknowledge that society today is more complex and less governable than a few decades ago, that insight does not automatically translate into the view that political structures are becoming obsolete instruments of governing. The analysis in this volume has had a more society-centered focus on complexity compared to some of our earlier work on governance (see for instance Pierre and Peters, 2000). Even so, our analysis differs from that of most society-centered governance scholars like Kooiman (1993, 2003) and Rhodes (1997) in that our focus is primarily on how governments deal with that complexity. We do not think that a diagnosis saying that society has become increasingly complex and, arguably, less governable automatically should result in a prescription that governance too should become messier. If anything, increasing complexity calls for increasing coordination and we argue that institutions are more apt at coordinating than, for instance, loose networks or partnerships.

Most importantly governments are better equipped to handle conflicts over interests and values than are the other institutions in society that have been proposed as alternative loci of governance. Markets are based on an assumption that buyers and sellers will coordinate, and that their interests are complementary rather than competitive. In most political situations there are competitive interests and there must be some means of reconciling those interests, or at least choosing among them. Similarly, networks either define away the existence of conflicting interests—if there is no agreement then there is no network—or there are limited mechanisms for resolving conflicts. Further, networks do not have the means of resolving conflicts in an open and democratic manner.

As well as resolving conflicts, governance represents the exercise of political power. In this conception "political" includes more than just the actions taken by and through the formal institutions of government and politics—often defined through political parties, legislatures, and the usual instrumentalities of liberal democracy. But similarly, political power exercised as a component of the governance process does not imply that those formal instrumentalities are worthless or ineffective. Rather, we are attempting to develop a nuanced understanding of governance and politics that involves both state and society, and their interaction, and which is also concerned with some fundamental political values such as democracy, conflict resolution, and accountability.

The analysis of governance is both an empirical and a normative enterprise. The values involved in governance are an essential basis from at which to start, and also to end, the discussion of how societies can govern themselves. While we have been discussing the capacity to govern and the need for the use of political power and authority, it is perhaps essential to consider the legitimate basis of the authority that is being employed. Governing can be easy, if all that is required is to exercise power and to implement decisions made by a small group of leaders and experts without careful consideration of the society, the diversity of the society, and the varying wants and demands of the public. Governing in a democratic and accountable manner is a more difficult process and requires a broader range of considerations, as well as the involvement of a broader array of actors.

Thus, any discussion of democratic governance must involve both some notions of achieving results and, at the same time, some notion of constraining the exercise of that power. The pursuit of that balance involves achieving a balance between two negative but contradictory images of government held by many people in society. On the one hand, government is seen as Leviathan, an unconstrained machine trampling on the interests of citizens in pursuit of its own ends, or perhaps the ends of an isolated elite holding power. Many critiques from both the political right and the political left have this sense of a powerful, bureaucratic government treading on the very people it is meant to serve.

On the other hand, government is also seen as a Gulliver, a seemingly powerful force that is constrained by countless small, but collectively powerful, threads (Hill, 1995). In the case of government institutions those threads can be the power that some groups in society are able to exercise over the policies that affect them. Governments are also severely constrained by the commitments made by previous governments that must be honored by the present regime, pension programs being an example with a great deal of contemporary relevance.

While both of these negative views have some validity, both also can be overcome through the effective design of policies (Ingram and Schneider, 1997) and institutions for governance (Sartori, 1994;

Sunstein, 2002). Many social scientists blanch when the word "design" is used, believing that governance is too complex for individuals to be able to design effectively,[1] there is yet a need to consider alternative means of achieving ends and acting prospectively to produce desired outcomes. It may be, however, that systems of governance are too important not to design, and instead of relying on incrementalism and good fortune there is a real need to consider creating design principles for governance, or at least aspects of governance.[2]

The importance of institutions

If those complex requirements for governance are to be fulfilled then effective institutions must be created and sustained. First, institutions are essential for overcoming the Gulliver image. If governments are to be able to make decisions, and especially if they are to be able to make high quality decisions involving significant technical content, high quality institutions will be needed. Likewise, if the decisions made by government are to result in coordinated and coherent policies, then there is a need for effective institutions that can make and enforce priorities (Painter, 1999). To perform their tasks of government the institutions of government must be capable of collecting information, providing the appropriate information to decision makers in a usable form, and resolving conflicts among social groups, as well as conflicts among elements of government itself.

Political and bureaucratic institutions must both be involved in the creation of these capacities for delivering governance. The political institutions must manage the internal conflicts that may arise as governments, especially in coalition governments in which multiple parties have contending ideas and contending searches for power. Those political institutions may also have to manage ministries and ministers who contend for budgetary resources, as well as find the means of making policies more coherent across a range of policy areas. Finally, there must be institutions that can manage the delivery of services to the public. Those institutions need not themselves deliver those services, but there will be a need for managing that implementation if it is to be provided through nongovernmental means.

Although perhaps not often discussed as an institutional problem per se effective governance also requires some means of linking the political and the permanent components of government. Different institutional political systems have found different means of getting civil servants and politicians to work together (Peters, 1987; Verheijen, 1999), but these solutions are always under pressure. Politicians often find the solutions to, in effect, bureaucratize policymaking, while permanent officials resent the meddling of "amateurs" in policy areas about which they generally have little expertise or even experience. There is, as in most political debates, some truth on both sides of this debate but governments must find ways of using the expertise of their permanent officials without those officials dominating policy and undermining democratic responsiveness of governments to the public.

The design for institutions for controlling democratically the political power, as well as the administrative power, created for governing is perhaps the more difficult task for governments. The powers of government can be awesome given the legal, financial, and administrative resources that are at its disposal; the Leviathan conception of government has all too much potential for being achieved in reality as well as in the popular myths about government. The potential for excess is of course most evident in authoritarian countries. If nothing else, governments have a monopoly over the legitimate use of force in society, and have the potential to abuse those powers, even in nominally democratic states. Governments also have a great deal of soft power, and if anything with the increasing capacities of the media to influence society the capacities of government have become even more awesome.

The tremendous powers at the disposal of the modern state require developing checks and balances. Some of those checks must be implemented at the level of policy formation, with the need to institutionalize channels of influence, and perhaps even to permit citizens to control many aspects of public policy that affect them most directly (Sorensen, 1997). Even when the clients, or the public as a whole, are not empowered to make decisions, effective democratic controls are needed to ensure that the decisions taken by government conform to the desires of the public, and perhaps more importantly that mechanisms for feedback exist to assess the impacts of policies on society.

The need to control governmental power is even more apparent as public policies are implemented. The old-fashioned concept of accountability remains a crucial question for governance, and accountability almost inherently involves the construction of institutions that can monitor what happens in the process of implementation and identify errors occurring in that process. To some extent that monitoring will involve the legislature, and the parliamentary forms of accountability that have been central to the Westminster system depend upon the executive reporting its action to parliament and defending those actions when challenged. In some political systems the legislature has developed committee systems that have been very successful in exercising oversight and enforcing accountability. Other institutions such as auditing organizations and the ombudsman also have been developed to hold the executive accountable for their actions.

While accountability is important as a means of punishing administrative malfeasance, for purposes of governing feedback may be a more important function for accountability institutions. Even in effective policy-making systems governments can and do make mistakes, and even if there are no policy disasters (Bovens and 't Hart, 1996) the policies may be suboptimal and can be made better. Further, as accountability regimens move in the direction of performance (Bouckaert, 1995) the feedback function becomes even more central to managing government and enforcing accountability. Further, this version of accountability can involve the public as well as formal institutional actors, although gauging performance and enforcing accountability will require constructing institutions.

Interinstitutional interaction in governance

The discussion of accountability in the previous section reflects the complexity of governance and the need to involve a number of institutions in the process of governing. Accountability reflects the need for horizontal coordination and interaction among institutions within a single level of government. The accountability issues mentioned emphasize the possibilities of designing interactions among institutions as mechanisms for control—the familiar checks and balances argument of presidential governments. Accountability is the most important of the interactions among institutions from a democratic perspective, but there are a number of other important interactions that affect governance.

The other central form of interaction at a single level of governance is coordination among actors in the delivery of services. We have emphasized throughout the volume the importance of priority setting in government, but once the multiple priorities are set there must be some means of making programs that may have contradictory, or even complementary, goals that function smoothly together. Achieving this coordination across programs is not easy given that most administration occurs within single ministries or agencies that may have a very narrow conception of priorities in governing and who may be unwilling to cooperate if that cooperation will diminish the possibilities of achieving goals within the program area.[3]

Vertical interactions among institutions are also important in achieving successful governance. Just as governance has come increasingly to involve interactions between state and societal actors so too it has come to involve complex vertical interactions with other levels of government. Intergovernmental relations have been important for governing for as long as there have been multiple levels of government (Wright, 1989), but the density of the interactions has begun to increase dramatically. One of the common strands of reform in countries around the world has been to decentralize governmental functions, and to create more complex systems of implementation (Bogason, 2000).

We have focused on the role of national level governments in much of our analysis but all levels of government are engaged in the same processes, albeit for different geographical areas and with different ranges of functions. These differences raise the problems of horizontal as well as vertical coordination of activities in governance. One of the criteria we have advanced for governance is that there should be some level of coherence among the activities of government(s). This criterion implies that when faced with the multiple and overlapping sources of governance, as well as multiple and potentially competing sources of policy and governance within each level of government, the governance system must develop institutional and procedural means for reducing contradictions, or perhaps even creating compatibility, among those sources of governance.

Relatively few governance systems have developed adequate means of coordinating vertically. This is especially true for federal systems, but even in unitary regimes the increasing investment in decentralizing reforms may reduce the degree of coherence and coordination in governance and in governing. At the extreme, countries such as France that have been argued to be governed from the center are now substantially more decentralized. Even before those reforms were implemented, however, the periphery had substantially greater influence than it would appear from examining the formal arrangements (Gremion, 1976). Governance there, as everywhere, involved negotiation and finding means of making potentially competing goals and political values compatible.

One of the more positive examples would be the cooperative federalism that exists in Germany. In contrast to the more disorganized federalism in the US and to some extent Canada, the German system permits coordination of fiscal policy among the levels of government, and utilizes common laws for a wide range of public functions. In addition, common civil service laws help to coordinate some aspects of implementation, albeit certainly not all. This *Politikverflechtung* (see Scharpf *et al.*, 1976) is a central aspect for governance within Germany. Other federal systems such as Australia also provide the means for coordinating policies and negotiating among themselves.

When there are no formalized institutional means such as those in some federal systems for generating greater coherence in policy, then the system devolves into bargaining and negotiation. While these methods may produce acceptable outcomes for the parties involved, they often become simply means for the more powerful actors to impose their demands on the other actors. In these settings governance becomes not so much a negotiated outcome among partners as a mechanism for using power.

Governing is not easy, and governance remains a scarce commodity. We have demonstrated that although governance systems have attempted to deal with the complexity of contemporary social and political life there are numerous pitfalls. Some of those pitfalls arise within the state itself, but some also arise from the interactions of state and society that are sometimes assumed to solve the problems created by formal means of government. Thus, individuals and institutions responsible for the design and implementation of governance systems face the continuing challenges of coping with a complex world, and perhaps the insatiable demands of the occupants of that world.

Notes

2 Toward a Theory of Governance

1. Some of this same reality may be evident in other Northern European states such as Denmark. See Togeby, 2003.

3 Governance: A Garbage Can Perspective

1. The use of the word appropriate here is deliberate, representing the influence of the (March and Olsen, 1989) "logic of appropriateness" as a basis of institutions.
2. These rationalist assumptions are perhaps clearest in the international relations literature that has focused on the state as a unitary actor pursuing its goals—Allison's rational actor (1971) model. Even in the domestic politics literature, however, there is sometimes a tendency to anthropomophize the state.
3. See also Richardson (2001) for a brief application of some of these ideas to the EU.
4. Nelson contrasted the success of government in getting a man on the moon with the lack of success in dealing with the social problems of the ghetto. The former involved using a known, if highly complex, technology, while the latter task could use no known technology and hence was a much more challenging task for government.
5. For a discussion of the differences between success from policy and political perspectives see Bovens *et al.* (2001).
6. More continuous participation in decision making may, it could be argued, tend to make preferences more consistent across the system. For one thing, the need to continue to participate in what is an iterative game may force actors to moderate their views and to cooperate more.
7. More accurately there may have been a period in which reformers believed that they could transform complex and often chaotic systems of governing into more rational, planned systems. The captivation of reformers with techniques such as PPBS and indicative planning were examples of the pursuit for rationality and efficiency.
8. Devices such as performance management that are central to contemporary management reforms are more akin to incremental solutions of trial and error than they are to rational planning systems (see Bouckaert, 1995).
9. We have made the similar argument (Peters, 1992; Peters and Pierre, 2004) that the EU and its governance arrangements tend to become bureaucratic politics in the face of the need to steer in a complex and largely unstructured situation.

4 Governance and Governability: Time, Space, and Structure

1. The conventional political science process model of policy and governing assumes that the process begins with problem identification and agenda setting and proceeds through implementation and evaluation. The feedback loop in the model provides for the continuity of the process but the assumption tends to be that it will begin again at the stage of agendas.

2. The historical institutionalist conceptions of path dependency and punctuated equilibrium come into play here.

3. There is some danger of tautology in more simplistic conceptions of governance and the policy process. That is: "Policy changes because of political pressures. How do we know there were political pressures? Because the policy changed."

4. Although some of the desire of governments to reform may be a function of public pressure, some also represents the power of ideologies held by elites and the power of ideas associated with the "New Public Management."

5. This is one aspect of the general paradox that we find existing within much of the literature of governance that comments on the movement away from the conventional hierarchical methods of governing.

6. This is a statement of the familiar bureaucratic politics argument. For the EU see Peters (1992).

7. This is the argument from Kornhauser (1959) that has to some extent been forgotten in the discussion of social capital.

8. In another context, Theodore Lowi's ideas of failures inherent in American "interest group liberalism" represent a contending view in which the public interest is captured by interest groups seeking highly differentiated benefits for their members.

9. This version of linkage also tends to favor the more powerful who are capable of influencing legislation and regulation at the expense of the less powerful. Institutions have been devised to attempt to overcome that bias in network-based policy making, but are for the most part ineffective.

10. Deviation as used here does not imply any normative element but rather simply that there are marked variations from what might be expected in linear, rationalist decision-making pattern.

11. A more general argument could be made about internationalization of processes. The arguments that these changes in governing inherently weaken domestic governments appear not to notice that national governments become the major players in the international policy arena, simply because no one else can. See Hirst (2000).

12. We would again argue that the Commission should not be seen as an integrated structure but rather as an aggregation of more or less autonomous directorates general, each using the policy to pursue its own views of policy and its bureaucratic interests.

13. Perhaps especially the EU (Olsen, 2001; Richardson, 2001).
14. Of course, one may wish not to maintain representative democracy and instead move toward more direct forms of citizen involvement and "deliberative democracy." While laudable on normative grounds, deliberative and networked models of governing may have some rather perverse unintended consequences for governing.

5 Multilevel Governance: A Faustian Bargain?

1. As with the governance debate taken more generally, the relative influence of British scholars in these debates has meant that pronouncements of the alarmed discovery of multiple power centers in governments has occurred from the perspective of what, in contemporary terms, is an unusually centralized regime.
2. For much of its history the power of the PRI tended to reduce the autonomy of the states and to centralize what might appear to be a rather decentralized federation. With the decline of Partido Revolucionario Institucional (PRI) power and state governments elected from opposition parties there has been more genuine decentralization of power (Velasco Cruz, 1999).

7 Governance, Accountability, and Democratic Legitimacy

1. This term was used by Yehezkel Dror (1986) to point to the need for some form of central direction in governing.
2. This problem is perhaps typified by Tilly's discussion of "the contentious French."
3. For a discussion of policy success and failure see Bovens *et al.* (2001).
4. There are also some questions about the performance of the EU as a governing organization. See Peters (2000c).
5. On the other hand, these difficult policy decisions represent the capacity to govern even in the face of potentially powerful public opposition (Ross, 2000).

8 Conclusion: Governance and Political Power

1. In political science and economics the concepts of bounded rationality and incrementalism emphasize the difficulty, or impossibility, of design. That having been said, however, design is necessary as new problems must be addressed, new technologies become available, and levels of interaction among public and private sector organizations must be managed.
2. See, for example, one attempt to create an approach to governance that enhances the possibilities for central direction in what had been a very decentralized system (Bouckaert *et al.*, 2000; Ministerial Working Group, 2002).

3. Changes in accountability toward performance standards may make achieving the coordination even more difficult. If organizations and their managers are to be judged on the extent to which they achieve predetermined policy targets then those actors may be unwilling to share their resources in order to achieve broader, crosscutting goals.

References

Allison, G. T. (1971), *Essence of Decision* (Boston, MA: Little, Brown).

Almond, G. (1988), "The Return of the State," *American Political Science Review*, 82:853–74.

Anderson, C. W. (1968), *The Political Economy of Modern Spain* (Madison: University of Wisconsin Press).

Anderson, J. (1990), "The 'New Right,' Enterprise Zones and Urban Development Zones," *International Journal of Urban and Regional Research*, 14:468–89.

Ashford, D. E. (1982), *French Pragmatism and British Dogmatism: Central–Local Policymaking in the Welfare State* (London: George Allen & Unwin).

Ashford, D. E. (ed.) (1990), *Discretionary Politics: Intergovernmental Social Transfers in Eight Countries* (Greenwich, CT: JAI Press).

Aucoin, P. and R. Heintzman (2000), "The Changing Nature of Political Accountability," in B. G. Peters and D. J. Savoie (eds), *Revitalizing the Public Service* (Montreal: McGill/Queens University Press).

Barberis, P. (1998), "The New Public Management and a New Accountability," *Public Administration*, 76:451–70.

Bauer, R. A. and H. Gergen (1968), *The Study of Policy Formation* (New York: Free Press).

Beauregard, R. A. and J. Pierre (2000), "Disputing the Global: A Skeptical View of Locality-based International Initiatives," *Policy and Politics*, 28:465–78.

Bemelmans-Videc, M. -L., R. C. Rist and E. Vedung (1998), *Carrots, Sticks and Sermons: Policy Instruments and Their Evaluation* (New Brunswick, NJ: Transaction Books).

Bendor, J., T. M. Moe, and K. W. Shotts (2001), "Recycling the Garbage Can: An Assessment of a Research Program," *American Political Science Review*, 95:169–90.

Bennett, D. (1995), "The Process of Harmonization Under NAFTA," *New Solutions*, 6:91–5.

Birch, A. H. (1984), "Overload, Ungovernability and Delegitimation: The Theories and the British Case," *British Journal of Political Science*, 14:135–60.

Bok, D. (1997), "Measuring the Performance of Government," in J. S. Nye, P. Zelikow, and D. C. King (eds), *Why People Don't Trust Government* (Cambridge, MA: Harvard University Press).

Börzel, T. and T. Risse (2002), "Network Governance and the European Union" (paper presented at Conference on Transformation of Governance in Globalized Society, University of Toronto).

Boston, J. (1994) "Purchasing Policy Advice: The Limits to Contracting Out," *Governance*, 7:1–30.

Bouckaert, G. (1995), "Improving Performance Measurement," in A. Halachmi and G. Bouckaert (eds), *The Enduring Challenges in Public Management, Surviving and Excelling in a Changing World* (San Francisco, CA: Jossey Bass).

Bouckaert, G. and A. Halachmi (1995), *Public Productivity through Quality and Productivity Management* (Amsterdam: IOS Press).

Bovens, M. A. P., P. 't Hart, and B. G. Peters (eds) (2001), *Success and Failure in Governance* (Cheltenham: Edward Elgar).

Bulmer, S. (1993), "The Governance of the European Union: A New Institutionalist Approach," *Journal of Public Policy*, 13:351–80.

Campbell, J. L. and O. K. Pedersen (2001), *The Rise of Neoliberalism and Institutional Analysis* (Princeton, NJ: Princeton University Press).

Chapman, R. A. (2000), *Public Sector Ethics for the New Millennium* (Aldershot: Ashgate).

Cohen, M., J. G. March and J. P. Olsen (1972), "A Garbage Can Model of Decision-making," *Administrative Science Quarterly*, 17:1–25.

Crozier, M. (1979), *On ne change pas la societe par decret* (Paris: B. Grasset).

Crozier, M., J. Watanuki, and S. Huntington (1975), *The Crisis of Democracy* (New York: New York Press).

Cyert, R. and J. G. March (1963), *A Behavioral Theory of the Firm* (Englewood Cliffs, NJ: Prentice-Hall).

Dahrendorf, R. (1960), "Effectiveness and Legitimacy: On the 'Governability' of Democracies," *The Political Quarterly*, 51:393–410.

Dalton, R. and B. Wattenberg (2000), *Politics Without Partisans* (Oxford: Oxford University Press).

Daujberg, C. and D. Marsh (1998), "Explaining Policy Outcomes: Integrating the Policy Network Approach with Macro and Micro Level Analysis," in D. Marsh (ed.), *Comparing Policy Networks* (Buckingham: Open University Press).

Deutsch, K. (1967), *The Nerves of Government* (New York: Free Press).

Dimaggio, P. and W. Powell (1991), "The Iron Cage Revisited: Institutional Isomorphism and Collective Rationality in Organizational Fields," *American Sociological Review*, 48:147–60.

Dogan, M. (1999), "Déficit de confiance dans les démocraties avancées," *Revue internationale de politique comparée*, 6:510–47.

Dror, Y. (1986), *Policymaking Under Adversity* (New Brunswick, NJ: Transaction).

Dyson, K. F. (1980), *The State Tradition in Western Europe* (Oxford: Oxford University Press).

Easton, D. (1965), *A Framework for Political Analysis* (Englewood Cliffs, NJ: Prentice-Hall).

Etzioni, A. (1995), *New Communitarian Thinking* (Charlottesville, VA: University Press of Virginia).

Evans, P. (1995), *Embedded Autonomy: States and Industrial Transformation* (Princeton, NJ: Princeton University Press).

Evans, P. (1997), "The Eclipse of the State? Reflections on Stateness in an Era of Globalization," *World Politics*, 50:62–87.

Evans, R. and A. Harding (1997), "Regionalisation, Regional Institutions and Economic Development," *Policy and Politics*, 25:19–30.

Fry, E. H. (1998), *The Expanding Role of State and Local Governments in U.S. Foreign Affairs* (New York: Council on Foreign Relations Press).

Gormley, W. T. (1983), *The Politics of Public Utility Regulation* (Pittsburgh, PA: University of Pittsburgh Press).

Grande, E. (1996), "The State and Interest Groups in the Context of Multi-level Decision-making: The Case of the European Union," *Journal of European Public Policy*, 3:318–38.

Gremion, P. (1976), *Le pouvoir peripherique* (Paris: Harmattan).

Gruber, J. E. (1992), *Controlling Bureaucracies: Dilemmas in Democratic Governance* (Berkeley, CA: University of California Press).

Gurr, T. R. and D. S. King (1987), *The State and the City* (Basingstoke: Macmillan).

Gustafsson, G. (1987), *Decentralisering av Politisk Makt* [Decentralization of Political Power] (Stockholm: Carlssons).

Harding, A. (1998), "Public–Private Partnerships in the UK," in J. Pierre (ed.), *Partnerships in Urban Governance: European and American Experiences* (London: Macmillan and New York: St. Martin's Press), 71–92.

Harding, A. and P. Le Gales (1998), "Cities and States in Europe," *West European Politics*, 21:120–45

Hay, C. (1998), "The Tangled Webs We Weave: The Discourse, Strategy and Practice of Networking," in D. Marsh (ed.), *Comparing Policy Networks* (Buckingham: Open University Press).

Hayes, M. T. (1992), *Incrementalism and Public Policy* (New York: Longman).

Hayward, J. E. S. (1983), *Governing the One and Divisible Republic* (London: Weidenfeld and Nicolson).

Hayward, J. E. S. (1986), *The State and the Market Economy: Industrial Patriotism and Economic Intervention in France* (New York: New York University Press).

Heimer, C. and A. Stinchcombe (1999), "Remodeling the Garbage Can: Implications of the Origins of Issues," in M. Egeberg and P. Laegreid (eds), *Organizing Political Institutions: Essays in Honor of Johan P. Olsen* (Oslo: Universitetsforlaget).

Heisler, M. O. (1974), "The European Policy Model," in Heisler (ed.), *Politics in Western Europe* (New York: David McKay).

Hill, L. (1995), "Is American Bureaucracy an Immobilized Gulliver or a Reganerative Phoenix?" *Administration and Society*, 27:322–60.

Hirst, P. Q. (2000), "Globalization and Democratization" (paper presented at the International Political Science Association Conference in Quebec City, Canada, August 1–5).

Hobbs, H. H. (1994), *City Hall Goes Abroad: The Foreign Policy of Local Politics* (Thousand Oaks, CA and London: Sage).

Holmberg, S. and L. Weibull (1998), *Opinionssamhället* [The Opinion Society](Gothenburg: SOM Institutet, University of Gothenburg).

Hood, C. (1986), *The Tools of Government* (Chatham, NJ: Chatham House).

Hood, C. (1991), "A Public Management for All Seasons?" *Public Administration*, 69:3–19.

Horwitz, R. B. (1986), "Understanding Deregulation," *Theory and Society*, 15:139–74.

Hufbauer, G. C. *et al.* (2000), *NAFTA and the Environment: Seven Years Later* (Washington, DC: Institute of International Economics).

Hunold, C. (2001), *Deliberative Democracy and Facility Siting* (Westport, CT: Praeger).

Huntington, S. P. (1966), *Political Order in Changing Societies* (New Haven, CT: Yale University Press).

Jessop, R. (2001), "Governance Failures in Multi-Level Governance" (paper presented at a Conference on Multi-Level Governance, Political Economy Research Centre, University of Sheffield, June).

Johnson, C. (1982), *MITI and the Japanese Miracle* (Stanford, CA: Stanford University Press).

Jones, B. D. (2001), *Politics and the Architecture of Choice* (Chicago: University of Chicago Press).

Jones, C. O. (1982), *The United States Congress: People, Place and Policy* (Homewood, IL: Dorsey).

Jones, C. O. (1984), *An Introduction to the Policy Process* (Monterey, CA: Brooks/Cole).

Jordan, A. (2001), "The European Union: An Evolving System of Multi-Level Governance . . . or Government?" *Policy and Politics*.

Jordan, A. G. and K. Schubert (1992), "A Preliminary Ordering of Policy Network Labels," *European Journal of Political Research*, 21:7–27.

Kagan, R. (2001), *Adversary Legalism: The American Way of Law* (Cambridge, MA: Harvard University Press).

Kassim, H., B. G. Peters, and V. Wright (eds) (2000), *European Union Policy Coordination: The National Dimension* (Oxford: Oxford University Press).

Kaufman, D. (2004), *Governance Redux: The Empirical Challenge* (Washington, D.C: World Bank).

Keating, M. (1992), *Comparative Urban Politics* (Cheltenham: Edward Elgar).

Keating, M. (1998), *The New Regionalism in Western Europe* (Cheltenham: Edward Elgar).

Kenworthy, L. (1995), *In Search of National Economic Success* (Beverly Hills, CA: Sage).

Kickert, W. J. M. (1997), "Public Governance in the Netherlands: An Alternative to Anglo-American Managerialism," *Public Administration*, 75:731–52.

Kjaer, A. M. (2004), *Governance* (Cambridge: Polity).

Klitgaard, R. E. (1988), *Controlling Corruption* (Berkeley, CA: University of California Press).

Kingdon, J. (1995), *Agendas, Alternatives and Public Policies* (2nd edn) (New York: Harper/Collins).

Knill, C. (1998), "European Policies: The Impact of National Administrative Traditions," *Journal of Public Policy*, 18:1–28.

Kohler-Koch, B. (1996), "Catching-up with Change: The Transformation of Governance in the EU," *Journal of European Public Policy*, 3:359–81.

Kohler-Koch, B. (2000), "Framing: The Bottleneck of Constructing Legitimate Institutions," *Journal of European Public Policy*, 7:512–31.

Kooiman, J. (1993), "Social-Political Governance: Introduction", in J. Kooiman (ed.), *Modern Governance: New Government-Society Interactions* (Newbury Park, CA: Sage).

Kooiman, J. (2003), *Governing as Governance* (London: Sage).

Kornhauser, W. (1959), *The Politics of Mass Society* (Glencoe, IL: Free Press).

Kraemer, P. E. (1968), *The Societal State* (Amsterdam: Bloom).

Krauss, E. S. and J. Pierre (1993), "Targeting Resources for Industrial Change," in B. A. Rockman and R. K. Weaver (eds), *Do Institutions Matter?: Government Capabilities in the United States and Abroad* (Washington, DC: The Brookings Institution), 151–86.

Kristensen, O. P. and L. N. Johansen (1983), "Corporatist Traits in Denmark, 1946–1976," in G. Lehmbruch and P. C. Schmitter (eds), *Patterns of Corporatist Policy-Making* (Beverly Hills, CA: Sage).

Leach, R. and J. Percy-Smith (2000), *Local Governance in Britain* (Basingstoke: Palgrave).

Le Galès, P. and C. Lequesne (eds) (1998), *Regions in Europe* (London: Routledge).

Lipset, S. M. (1959), "Some Social Requisites of Democracy: Economic Development and Political Legitimacy," *American Political Science Review*, 53.

Lowndes, V. (forthcoming), "Urban Politics and Institutional Theory," in B. G. Peters, J. Pierre, and G. Stoker (eds), *Assessing Institutionalism*.

Mann, M. (1997), "Has Globalization Ended the Rise and Rise of the Nation State?" *Review of International Political Economy*, 4:477–96.

March, J. G. and J. P. Olsen (1976), *Ambiguity and Choice in Organizations* (Bergen: Norwegian University Press).

March, J. G. and J. P. Olsen (1989), *Rediscovering Institutions: The Organizational Basis of Politics* (New York: Free Press).

March, J. G. and J. P. Olsen (1995), *Democratic Governance* (New York: Free Press).

March, J. G. and H. A. Simon (1957), *Organizations* (New York: John Wiley).

Marks, G., L. Hooghe and K. Blank (1996), "European Integration from the 1980s: State-Centric v. Multi-Level Governance," *Journal of Common Market Studies*, 34:343–77.

Markusen, A. (1987), *Regions: The Economics and Politics of Territory* (Totowa, NJ: Rowman & Littlefield Publishers).

Marsh, D. and R. A. W. Rhodes (eds) (1992a), *Policy Networks in British Government* (Oxford: Clarendon Press).

Marsh, D. and R. A. W. Rhodes (1992b), *Implementing Thatcherite Policies* (Buckingham: Open University Press).

May, P. and S. Winter (1999), "Regulatory Enforcement in Danish Agriculture," *Journal of Public Policy Analysis and Management*.

Migdal, J. S. (1988), *Strong Societies and Weak States: State Society Relations and State Capacity in the Third World* (Princeton, NJ: Princeton University Press).

Ministry of Finance (1998), *Borgerne og den offentlige sektor* [Citizens and the Public Sector](Copenhagen: Finansministeriet).

Mitchell, J. M. and W. C. Mitchell (1969), *Political Analysis & Public Policy* (Chicago, IL: Rand McNally).

Montin, S. (1994), *Swedish Local Government in Transition* (Orebro: Department of Social Sciences, University of Orebro).

Mulgan, R. (2000), " 'Accountability': An Ever-expanding Concept?" *Public Administration*, 78:555–73.

Navari, C. (1991), "On the Withering Away of the State," in C. Navari (ed.), *The Condition of States* (Milton Keynes: Open University Press), 143–66.

Nelson, R. (1968), *The Moon and the Ghetto* (New York: Norton).

Newman, P. (2000), "Changing Patterns of Regional Governance in the EU," *Urban Studies*, 37:895–908.

Newton, K. and M. Kaase (eds) (1996), *Beliefs in Government* (Oxford: Oxford University Press).

Norris, P. (ed.) (1996), *Critical Citizens* (Oxford: Oxford University Press).

Nurmi, H. (1998), *Rational Behavior and the Design of Institutions* (Cheltenham: Edward Elgar).

Nye, J. S., P. D. Zelikow, and D. C. King (1997), *Why People Don't Trust Government* (Cambridge, MA: Harvard University Press).

Offe, C. (1985), *Disorganized Capitalism* (Cambridge, MA: MIT Press).

Okimoto, D. (1988), *Between MITI and the Market* (Stanford, CA: Stanford University Press).

Olsen, J. P. (1987), *Organized Democracy* (Oslo: Universitetsforlaget).

Olsen, J. P. (2001), "Garbage Cans, New Institutionalism and the Study of Politics," *American Political Science Review*, 95:191–98.

Olsen, J. P. and B. G. Peters (1996), *Lessons from Experience: Experiential Learning in Administrative Reform in Eight Countries* (Oslo: Universitetsforlaget).

Osborne, D. and E. Gaebler (1991), *Reinventing Government* (Reading, MA: Addison-Wesley).

Padgett, J. F. (1980), "Managing Garbage Can Hierarchies," *Administrative Science Quarterly*, 25:583–602.

Painter, M. (2001), "Multi-level Governance and the Emergence of Collaborative Federal Institutions in Australia," *Policy and Politics*, 29:137–50.

Payne, A. (2000), "Globalization and Regionalist Governance," in J. Pierre (ed.), *Debating Governance* (Oxford: Oxford University Press), 201–18.

Pempel, T. J. and K. Tsunekawa (1979), "Corporatism Without Labor? The Japanese Anomaly," in P. C. Schmitter and G. Lehmbruch (eds), *Trends Toward Corporatist Intermediation* (Beverly Hills, CA, and London: Sage).

Perez-Diaz, V. (1995), *The Return of Civil Society* (Cambridge, MA: Harvard University Press).

Peters, B. G. (1991), *The Politics of Taxation* (Oxford: Blackwells).

Peters, B. G. (1992), "Bureaucratic Politics in the European Union," in A. M. Sbragia (ed.), *Euro-Politics* (Washington, DC: The Brookings Institution).

Peters, B. G. (1999), "Managing Horizontal Government: The Politics of Networks," *Public Administration*, 76:295–312.

Peters, B. G. (2000a), "Governance and Comparative Politics," in J. Pierre (ed.), *Debating Governance: Authority, Steering, and Democracy* (Oxford: Oxford University Press), 36–53.

Peters, B. G. (2000b), "Managing Horizontal Government" (paper presented at Conference on Improving Policy Coherence, Taipei, Taiwan, July 4–5).

Peters, B. G. (2000c), "Is There an Implementation Deficit in the European Union?" in N. Nugent (ed.), *At the Heart of the Union* (2nd edn) (Basingstoke: Macmillan).

Peters, B. G. (2000d), "Contracts as a Tool of Public Management, in Y. Fortin (ed.), *La contractualisation dans le secteur public des pays industrialisés depuis 1980* (Paris: L'Harmattan).

Peters, B. G. (2001a), *The Future of Governing: Four Emerging Models* (2nd edn) (Lawrence, KS: University Press of Kansas).

Peters, B. G. (2001b), "Prefectoral Government", in *New Encyclopedia of the Social Sciences* (London: Elsevier).

Peters, B. G. and J. Pierre (1998), "Governance without Government: Rethinking Public Administration", *Journal of Public Administration Research and Theory*, 8:223–42.

Peters, B. G. and J. Pierre (2004), "Multi-level Government—A Faustian Bargain?," in Bache, I. and M. Flinders (eds), *Multi-Level Governance* (Oxford: Oxford University Press).

Peters, B. G., R. A. W. Rhodes, and V. Wright (2000), *Administering the Summit* (London: Macmillan).

Peters, B. G. and D. J. Savoie (1998), *Taking Stock* (Montreal: McGill/Queens University Press).

Peters, B. G. and F. Van Nispen (eds) (1998), *Policy Instruments and Public Policy* (Cheltenham: Edward Elgar).

Pierre, J. (1994), *Den lokala staten. Studier av den kommunala självstyrelsens förutsättningar och restriktioner* [The Local State: Studies on the preconditions and restrictions on local autonomy] (Stockholm: Almqvist & Wiksell).

Pierre, J. (ed.) (1998), *Partnerships in Urban Governance: European and American Experiences* (Basingstoke: Macmillan).

Pierre, J. (ed.) (2000), *Debating Governance: Authority, Steering, and Democracy* (Oxford: Oxford University Press).

Pierre, J. and B. G. Peters (2000), *Governance, Politics and the State* (Basingstoke: Macmillan).

Pierre, J. and B. G. Peters (2001), "Recent Developments in Intergovernmental Relationships: Towards Multi-Level Governance," *Policy and Politics*, 29:131–5.

Pierre, J. and G. Stoker (2000), "Towards Multi-Level Governance," in P. Dunleavy *et al.* (eds), *Developments in British Politics* (6th edn) (Basingstoke: Macmillan), 29–46.

Pierson, P. (1994), *Dismantling the Welfare State?* (Cambridge: Cambridge University Press).

Polanyi, K. (1942), *The Great Transformation* (New York: Farrar & Rinehart).

Polidano, M. (1997), "The Bureaucrat Who Fell Under a Bus: Ministerial Responsibility, Executive Agencies and the Derek Lewis Affair in Britain," *Governance*, 12:201–31.

Pollitt, C. and G. Bouckaert (2000), *Public Management Reform: A Comparative Analysis* (Oxford: Oxford University Press).

Pressman, J. L. and A. Wildavsky (1974), *Implementation* (Berkeley, CA: University of California Press).

Putnam, R. D., R. Leonardi and R. V. Nanetti (1993), *Making Democracy Work: Civic Tradition in Modern Italy* (Princeton, NJ: Princeton University Press).

Reigner, H. (2001), "Multi-level Governance or Co-administration? Transformation and Continuity in French Local Government," *Policy and Politics*, 29:181–92.

Rhodes, R. A. W. (1986), *The National World of Local Government* (London: Allen & Unwin).

Rhodes, R. A. W. (1997), *Understanding Governance: Policy Networks, Governance, Reflexivity and Accountability* (Buckingham: Open University Press).

Rhodes, R. A. W., P. Weller, and H. Bakvis (eds) (1997), *Managing the Hollow Crown: Countervailing Tendencies in Core Executives* (New York: St. Martin's Press).

Richardson, J. J. (2001), "Policy-making in the EU: Interests, Ideas and Garbage Cans of Primeval Soup," in J. J. Richardson (ed.), *European Union: Power and Policy-making* (2nd edn) (London: Routledge).

Rockman, B. (1998), "The Changing Role of the State," in B. G. Peters and D. J. Savoie (eds), *Taking Stock: Assessing Public Sector Reforms* (Montreal and Kingston: McGill-Queen's University Press), 20–44.

Rokkan, S. (1966), "Norway: Numerical Democracy and Corporate Pluralism," in R. A. Dahl (ed.), *Political Oppositions in Western Democracies* (New Haven, CT: Yale University Press).

Rose, R. and B. G. Peters (1976), *Can Government Go Bankrupt?* (New York: Basic Books).

Rosenau, J. N. (2001), "The Demand for Governance" (paper presented at International Conference on Multi-Level Governance, University of Sheffield, June).

Rosenau, J. N. and E.-O. Czempiel (eds) (1992), *Governance without Government: Order and Change in World Politics* (Cambridge and New York: Cambridge University Press).

Ross, F. (2000), "Interests and Choice in the 'Not Quite So New' Politics of Welfare," *West European Politics*.

Salamon, L. (2000), *Handbook of Policy Instruments* (New York: Oxford University Press).

Salamon, L. (2001), "Introduction," in L. Salamon (ed.), *The Tools of Public Action* (New York: Oxford University Press).

Salamon, L. (2002), *Handbook of Policy Instruments* (New York: Oxford University Press).

Savoie, D. J. (1994), *Reagan, Thatcher, Mulroney: In Search of A New Bureaucracy* (Pittsburgh, PA: University of Pittsburgh Press).

Schaap, L. and M. J. W. Van Twist (1997), "The Dynamics of Closedness in Networks," in W. J. M. Kickert, E. -H. Klijn, and J. F. M. Koppenjan (eds), *Managing Complex Networks* (London: Sage).

Scharpf, F. (1997), "Introduction: The Problem-Solving Capacity of Multi-Level Governance," *Journal of European Public Policy*, 4:520–38.

Scharpf, F. W. (1988), "The Joint-Decision Trap: Lessons from German Federalism and European Integration," *Public Administration*, 66:239–78.

Scharpf, F. W., B. Reissert, and F. Schnabel (1976), *Politikverflechtung* (Konigsburg: Scriptor).

Schmitter, P. C. (1974), "Still the Century of Corporatism?" *Review of Politics*, 36:85–131.

Schon, D. A. and M. Rein (1994), *Frame Reflection* (Cambridge, MA: MIT Press).

Schumpeter, J. (1947), *Capitalism, Socialism and Democracy* (New York: Harper & Bros).

Sharpe, L. J. (1988), "The Growth and Decentralisation of the Modern State," *European Journal of Political Research*, 16:365–80.

Simeon, R. and D. Cameron (2000), "Intergovernmental Realtions and Democratic Citizenship," in B. G. Peters and D. J. Savoie (eds), *Governance in the 21st Century* (Montreal: McGill/Queeens University Press).

Simon, H. A. (1947), *Administrative Behavior* (New York: Free Press).

Smith, A. (1997), "Studying Multi-Level Governance: Examples from French Translations of the Structural Funds," *Public Administration*, 20:711–29.

Smyrl, M. E. (1997), "Does European Community Regional Policy Empower the Regions?," *Governance*, 10:287–309.

Sorensen, E. (1997), "Democracy and Empowerment," *Public Administration*, 75:553–67.

Stoker, G. (1998), "Governance as Theory: Five Propositions," *International Social Science Journal*, 155:17–28.

Strömberg, L. and J. Westerståhl (eds) (1984), *De nya kommunerna* [The New Municipalities] (Stcokholm: Liber).

Taggart, P. A. (1996), *The New Populism and the New Politics* (London: Macmillan).

Tarrow, S. (1998), *Power in Movement: Social Movements and Contentious Politics* (2nd edn) (Cambridge: Cambridge University Press).

Thomas, P. G. (1998), "The Changing Nature of Accountability," in B. G. Peters and D. J. Savoie (eds), *Taking Stock: Assessing Public Sector Reforms* (Montreal and Kingston: McGill-Queen's University Press), 348–93.

Thompson, G., J. Frances, R. Levacic, and J. Mitchell (1991), *Markets, Hierarchies and Networks* (London: Sage).

Togeby, L. (2003), *Magt og Demokrati i Denmark: Hovedresultater fra Magtutredningen* [Power and Democracy in Denmark: The Main Results from the Power Commission](Aarhus: Aarhus Universitetsforlag).

in 't Veld, R. (1991), "Autopoesis, Configuration and Steering: Impossibility Therom or Dynamic Steering Theory," in in 't Veld *et al.* (eds), *Autopoesis and Configuration Theory* (Dordrect: Kluwer).

Van Waarden, F. (1995), "Persistence of National Policy Styles: A Study of their Institutional Foundations," in M. Unger and F. van Waarden (eds), *Convergence or Diversity: Internationalization and Economic Policy Response* (Aldershot: Avebury).

Velasco Cruz, J. L. (1999), *El debate actual sobre el federalismo mexicano* (Mexico DF: Instituto Mora).

Walker, D. (1999), *The Future of Federalism* (3rd edn) (New York: Chatham House).

Weaver, R. K. and B. A. Rockman (1993), *Do Institutions Matter?* (Washington, DC: The Brookings Institution.

Weiss, L. (1998), *The Myth of the Powerless State* (Cambridge: Cambridge University Press).

Weller, P., H. Bakvis and R. A. W. Rhodes (eds) (1997), *The Hollow Crown: Countervailing Trends in Core Executives* (New York: St. Martin's Press).

Woodside, K. (1998), "The Acceptability and Visibility of Policy Instruments," in B. G. Peters and F. K. M. van Nispen (eds), *Public Policy Instruments* (Cheltenham: Edward Elgar), 162–84.

Wright, D. S. (1989), *Intergovernmental Relations in the United States* (3rd edn) (Monterey, CA: Brooks/Cole).

Wright, V. (1998), "Intergovernmental Relations and Regional Government in Europe: A Sceptical View," in P. Le Galès and C. Lequesne (eds), *Regions in Europe* (London: Routledge), 39–49.

Wunder, B. (1995), *Les influences du "modele" Napoleonien d'administration sur l'organisation administrative des autres pays* (Brussels: IIAS, *Cahiers d'Histoire de l'Administration*), 4.

Zito, A. (1998), "Epistemic Communities and European Integration," Paper delivered at ECPR 26th Joint Sessions, Warwick, England, March.

Zito, A. R. (2000), *Creating Environmental Policy in the European Union* (New York: St. Martin's Press).

Index

Printed in the United States
R3440600002B/R34406PG202128BVX2B/1}/A